THE ENDURANCE FACTOR
THRIVING IN BUSINESS WHEN OTHERS QUIT

Sadia Watara

TABLE OF CONTENTS

PREFACE

Endurance is often misunderstood in the world of business. Many see it as merely holding on, as if survival were the only goal, but in truth endurance is about thriving where others falter. It is about seeing opportunity in difficulty, purpose in struggle, and reward in sacrifice. This book was born from years of observing entrepreneurs, leaders, and professionals who either succeeded beyond measure or gave up when the road grew too heavy. What I came to understand is that the difference between those who rise and those who surrender lies not in talent alone, nor in resources, nor in timing, but in endurance. It is endurance that builds resilience. It is endurance that nurtures creativity in hard times. It is endurance that keeps a vision alive when all signs seem to argue for retreat. When I set out to write The Endurance Factor, my intent was not to create a manual of clichés about persistence. Rather, my goal was to give a deeper understanding of why endurance is the master quality that determines longevity in business, and why those who cultivate it find themselves building not just companies but legacies. I wanted to show how endurance is not passive waiting but active thriving. It is the choice to press on with clarity when markets collapse, when funds run dry, when competitors seem stronger, and when doubt creeps in from every side. In business, endurance requires more than stamina. It requires conviction, adaptability, emotional intelligence, and a keen awareness that the hardest moments often conceal the seeds of the greatest opportunities. I have spoken with entrepreneurs who lost everything and yet found a new fire to build again. I have studied leaders who watched partners walk away, investors withdraw, and teams disband, yet who refused to abandon their vision and instead restructured, reinvented, and reclaimed their purpose. These individuals demonstrate the endurance factor in its purest form, showing that when others quit, thriving is still possible.

Writing this book has been both a challenge and a privilege. The challenge came in resisting the temptation to make endurance sound easy. It is not. Nothing of lasting worth in business comes without a price. Endurance often means sacrificing comfort, sleep, and even relationships. It means facing criticism from those who doubt your path and isolation from those who cannot see your vision. Yet it also brings extraordinary rewards. To endure is to discover inner strength that remains hidden until tested. To endure is to realize that failure is not the end but the soil in which reinvention takes root. To endure is to stand in the middle of storms and yet believe that sunlight is inevitable. This book is not written for the faint-hearted. It is written for the entrepreneur who has tasted both victory and defeat and longs for clarity on how to stay the course. It is for the leader who feels the weight of decision-making and fears the temptation to abandon the mission. It is for the dreamer who has faced rejection and yet senses that the dream still holds life. It is for the student of business who seeks to understand not only strategy and finance but the emotional and psychological backbone of enterprise. It is for anyone who wants to build a business that can outlast setbacks, survive economic downturns, and thrive in the face of adversity.

You will notice as you read that the book weaves together principles, case studies, and reflections. Each chapter carries both the intellectual and the emotional dimensions of endurance. I have avoided sterile theories because endurance is not abstract. It is lived. It is felt in the nights when an entrepreneur lies awake worrying about payroll. It is felt in the offices where leaders must deliver bad news yet still inspire hope. It is felt in the quiet moments of decision when giving up seems more rational than going on. Endurance is personal, and I wanted this book to speak directly to the human soul as much as it speaks to the business mind. In preparing this manuscript, I also revisited my own experiences. I remembered ventures that failed, partnerships that dissolved, and seasons where quitting seemed more attractive than pressing on. But I also remembered the breakthroughs that came after long waits, the victories that emerged after repeated setbacks, and the satisfaction of seeing ideas once mocked become celebrated. These memories reminded me that endurance is not only the foundation of business but also of life itself. To live fully is to endure. To endure is to thrive. If there is one message you take away from this book, let it be this: success is not only about what you start but about what you finish. The marketplace is full of talented beginners who never reach the end. True distinction belongs to those who endure. As you turn these pages, I invite you to walk with me through stories, lessons, and insights that will deepen your understanding of what it means to thrive in business when others quit. I hope you will find encouragement when discouraged, clarity when confused, and strength when weary. May you discover within yourself the endurance factor and may it carry you not only through the challenges of business but through the greater challenges of life.

FOREWORD

Business has always been a test of character as much as a test of skill. I have met countless people with brilliant ideas, access to capital, and promising strategies, yet their ventures collapsed because they lacked the grit to stay the course. On the other hand, I have watched individuals with fewer resources, fewer connections, and fewer advantages rise to heights that seemed improbable because they refused to quit. They pressed on in storms, adapted to shifting realities, and cultivated a strength that could not be bought. That strength is endurance, and it is the defining quality of those who thrive when others quit. When the author of this book approached me to write the foreword, I did not hesitate, because the message of The Endurance Factor could not be more relevant. We live in an era where entrepreneurship is glorified but often misunderstood. Social media highlights success stories without showing the nights of doubt, the years of delay, and the scars of rejection. Young entrepreneurs often think success is quick if the idea is good enough or if funding is sufficient. Yet history and experience tell another story. The entrepreneurs who build companies that last, the leaders who outlive crises, and the visionaries who leave legacies all share one thing in common: endurance.

This book is a timely and much-needed reminder that business is a marathon, not a sprint. It speaks to the truth that endurance is not passive waiting but active thriving. It shows that when the market shifts, endurance is what drives innovation. When capital dries up, endurance is what forces creativity. When criticism mounts, endurance is what keeps vision alive. Without endurance, even the most brilliant strategy collapses. With endurance, even the weakest beginnings can blossom into greatness. As you read through these chapters, you will be struck by the depth of insight and the humanity of the message. This is not a sterile textbook of principles, nor is it a romantic tale of overnight triumphs. It is an honest exploration of what it means to press forward when everything argues against you. The author does not shy away from the pain of endurance but also does not fail to highlight its reward. You will encounter stories that challenge you, principles that equip you, and reflections that inspire you. Most importantly, you will be reminded that success belongs not to the fastest nor the strongest but to those who endure to the end.

What I appreciate most about this book is that it speaks both to the experienced leader and the aspiring entrepreneur. If you are seasoned in business, you will find here a mirror that reflects your own battles and a compass that reminds you why you cannot quit. If you are just beginning, you will find a roadmap that will save you from the illusions of quick success and ground you in the realities of long-term achievement. Either way, this book will strengthen your resolve and shape your perspective. The author has captured the essence of endurance in a way that is both practical and profound. You will not only learn how to cultivate endurance but also why it matters, how it transforms challenges into opportunities, and how it separates temporary ventures from lasting enterprises. This book is not about surviving business. It is about thriving in business when others give up. That is the endurance factor, and that is why you must read every page with an open mind and a ready heart. As you begin this journey, prepare yourself for both reflection and action. Allow the words to challenge your fears, to strengthen your will, and to expand your vision. Let this book remind you that while many will quit when the road gets tough, you have the power to endure, to thrive, and to build something that lasts.

INTRODUCTION

Business is often described as a battlefield, a competition of strategy, innovation, and execution. Yet what is rarely acknowledged is that the true battlefield lies within. It is fought in the mind of the entrepreneur, in the heart of the leader, and in the spirit of the dreamer. It is not merely about outsmarting competitors or outpacing markets. It is about enduring when everything in you screams to give up. It is about holding on when every signal says let go. It is about thriving when the odds appear impossible. The truth is that most people quit. They quit not because they lack intelligence but because they lack endurance. They quit not because their ideas were poor but because their patience was thin. They quit not because the world closed its doors but because they refused to keep knocking. The difference between the few who rise to enduring success and the many who fade into obscurity lies in the ability to keep moving when it would be easier to stop. That is the endurance factor, and it is the heartbeat of this book. Every entrepreneur begins with passion. The early days are fueled by excitement and energy. But as time goes on, difficulties appear. Sales are slower than expected, investors hesitate, customers complain, competitors grow stronger, and doubt becomes louder. At this point, passion alone is not enough. Many quit. A few endure. Those who endure discover that hardship is not the end of the journey but the birthplace of resilience, innovation, and growth. This introduction serves as both a warning and an invitation. The warning is clear: if you cannot endure, you cannot thrive. The invitation is powerful: if you choose to endure, you can thrive even when others quit. This book will not teach you shortcuts to success because there are none. It will not flatter you with illusions of quick victories because those are rare and often unsustainable. Instead, it will guide you into the discipline, mindset, and strategies of endurance. In the chapters ahead, you will learn how endurance is cultivated, how it manifests in decision-making, and how it sustains leaders in the darkest seasons. You will discover that endurance is not only about surviving difficulties but about leveraging them for growth. You will see that when crises strike, endurance is what sparks reinvention. When failure comes, endurance is what allows a fresh start. When opportunities seem scarce, endurance is what keeps vision alive until new doors open.

Business is often described as a battlefield, a competition of strategy, innovation, and execution. Yet the truest battlefield is not found in boardrooms or stock markets. It is fought in the unseen places of the human spirit. It is fought in the determination of the entrepreneur who refuses to let go of a vision. It is fought in the resilience of the leader who holds a company together when storms are raging. It is fought in the heart of the dreamer who has faced countless rejections and yet still chooses to press forward. This battle is not against competitors alone. It is against fatigue, against doubt, against the silent whispers that suggest quitting would be easier. The capacity to win that battle is what separates those who endure from those who collapse. That capacity is the endurance factor, and it is the heartbeat of this book. The truth is harsh but necessary: most people quit. They quit not because they lack brilliance but because they lack resilience. They quit not because their vision is unworthy but because the cost is heavier than they expected. They quit not because the market closes its doors but because they do not want to keep knocking. The road of business is littered with unfinished projects, abandoned ventures, and forgotten ideas that might have changed the world had someone chosen to endure. Yet alongside these broken remnants, there stand stories of men and women who refused to give up, who pushed forward against incredible odds, and whose businesses not only survived but thrived in ways that seemed impossible. Their secret was not luck, not privilege, not connections, but endurance. Endurance in business is not blind persistence. It is not about stubbornly continuing down a path that is clearly destructive. Rather, it is about holding firmly to purpose while being willing to adapt methods. It is about having the courage to stay in the game when others leave but also the wisdom to pivot when circumstances demand it. Endurance is not stagnation. It is dynamic, evolving, and alive. It requires patience, vision, creativity, and emotional strength. It demands the ability to withstand seasons of scarcity, criticism, and even failure without losing the essence of the mission. At the beginning of every venture, enthusiasm is abundant. Ideas feel fresh, energy flows easily, and excitement is contagious. Investors may listen eagerly, customers may show interest, and friends may offer support. In those moments, endurance feels unnecessary because the journey seems smooth. But as time stretches forward, reality arrives. Delays creep in. Sales do not match projections. Partners disagree. Competitors move faster. Funding becomes scarce. Personal sacrifices mount. The glamour fades, and the grind begins. This is the stage where most people reconsider their choices. Many quit. A few endure. Those who endure discover that true business success is forged not in the moments of excitement but in the valleys of challenge. To endure is to see beyond immediate struggles into long-term possibilities. It is to look at setbacks and view them not as signs of failure but as part of the path. It is to wake up each morning with the willingness to try again even when yesterday ended in disappointment. It is to keep refining strategies, to keep reaching out to customers, to keep innovating, and to keep believing when others have written you off. Endurance allows you to transform rejection into feedback, scarcity into creativity, and obstacles into steppingstones. It transforms what seems unbearable into the very fuel that sustains progress. Endurance also shapes the leader. Without endurance, leadership is fragile because the pressure of decisions becomes overwhelming. With endurance, leadership becomes resilient because it understands that pressure is not a threat but a teacher. A leader who endures can carry the weight of responsibility without collapsing. They can inspire teams in seasons of loss, and they can model perseverance that filters down into every level of an organization. Such leadership is not born in times of ease but in seasons of resistance. Endurance is the furnace that strengthens leaders for the long haul. Many people look at successful businesses and see only the outcome. They see the expansion, the revenue, the recognition, and the polished image of victory. What they do not see are the countless moments of near collapse, the decisions made in tears, the days when giving up seemed more rational than pressing on. Behind every enduring business are stories of endurance that few will ever know. Behind every achievement lies a hundred hidden struggles. This book aims to uncover those realities so that you do not enter the business world with illusions of ease but with clarity about what it truly takes to thrive. One of the greatest misconceptions in business is the belief that success belongs to the most talented or the most well-connected. Talent and networks are valuable, but they cannot replace endurance. History is filled with talented individuals whose brilliance never translated into lasting achievement because they lacked the ability to endure. It is equally filled with individuals who did not appear exceptionally gifted or privileged yet built empires because they refused to quit. Endurance turns ordinary people into extraordinary builders. The endurance factor is also essential in times of failure. Failure is inevitable in business. Plans collapse. Products flop. Partnerships dissolve. No one escapes it. What matters is how one responds to it. Quitting interprets failure as the final word. Endurance interprets failure as a teacher, as feedback, as the soil of reinvention. The entrepreneurs who thrive are those who allow failure to instruct them rather than destroy them. They rise from ashes with lessons learned, strategies sharpened, and resolve strengthened. Their failures become steppingstones toward future success.

This book is not a celebration of suffering for its own sake. It is not about glorifying struggle as if hardship were desirable in itself. Rather, it is about recognizing that struggle is inevitable and that endurance is the only way to transform it into growth. Business is demanding. There will be sleepless nights, strained relationships, financial uncertainties, and emotional turmoil. Pretending otherwise is to set yourself up for disappointment. The endurance factor equips you to face those realities with strength and to emerge not broken but stronger, not bitter but wiser, not defeated but thriving. As you read, I want you to reflect on your own journey. What dreams have you left unfinished because the cost became too high? What opportunities slipped away because you grew weary of waiting? What visions did you abandon because failure convinced you they were impossible? This book is an invitation to reclaim them. It is a call to step back into the arena with renewed courage. It is a reminder that the path of endurance may be hard, but it is the only path that leads to greatness. The chapters that follow will not offer you shortcuts. They will offer you principles. They will not offer you illusions. They will offer you truth. They will not tell you it will be easy. They will tell you it will be worth it. You will encounter stories of entrepreneurs who endured where others quit, lessons on cultivating resilience, and strategies for transforming adversity into progress. You will be challenged to shift your mindset from seeking quick results to building long-term strength. You will be reminded that success is not merely about starting well but about finishing strong. The endurance factor is not only a business principle but a life principle. To endure is to thrive in every sphere. Whether in careers, relationships, health, or personal growth, the ability to press on when others give up determines the quality of one's journey. A life without endurance is fragile and easily broken. A life with endurance is powerful and deeply fulfilling. As you immerse yourself in this book, I encourage you to make endurance personal. Do not treat it as a concept to admire from a distance. Let it become a conviction that shapes your choices, your actions, and your vision. Let it become the foundation on which you build not just a business but a legacy. I wrote this book because endurance has been the difference-maker in my own journey and in the journeys of countless entrepreneurs I have studied. I wanted to strip away the illusions that business is easy or that success is guaranteed by talent. Instead, I wanted to highlight the one quality that unites every lasting enterprise: the refusal to quit. If you commit to reading this book with an open mind and an enduring spirit, I believe it will equip you with tools that go beyond business. The endurance factor is not only for entrepreneurs but for anyone who desires to live with resilience, persistence, and purpose. It is a mindset that will serve you in relationships, careers, personal growth, and every arena where challenges abound. As you step into this journey, I ask you to reflect deeply on your own path. Where have you been tempted to quit? What dreams have you abandoned too soon? What goals have you left unfinished because the struggle seemed too much? Let this book reawaken your conviction. Let it remind you that you are capable of more than you imagine. Let it equip you to press forward with strength. Endurance is not glamorous, but it is glorious. It is not easy, but it is necessary. It is not for the faint-hearted, but it rewards those who embrace it with victories that outlast time. This is the endurance factor, and it is yours to claim.

1

The Foundation of Endurance

Every enduring business begins not with a product or a service but with the unseen determination of its founder. Long before strategies are crafted, markets are tested, or profits are earned, there is a decision within the heart of an entrepreneur to remain when others walk away. The foundation of endurance is this decision to stand firm when storms arrive, to believe in the possibility of success when failure seems more likely, and to carry within oneself a vision strong enough to outlast disappointments. Many entrepreneurs fail not because their ideas lacked brilliance but because they surrendered at the point of resistance. Endurance is therefore not a luxury but the most critical pillar upon which businesses that last are built. It is easy to admire companies that have thrived for decades or entrepreneurs who have grown from nothing to empire builders yet hidden behind every story of success is a long narrative of nights filled with doubts, seasons of rejection, and moments where quitting would have seemed like the reasonable choice. The foundation of endurance is laid in these invisible struggles, and only those who choose to endure get the chance to see the results of their sacrifice. To understand this foundation, one must appreciate that entrepreneurship is rarely a smooth path. Every business, no matter how well planned, encounters moments of uncertainty. Customers change their preferences, markets shift without notice, capital runs dry, and even close allies sometimes walk away. It is in such times that the entrepreneur is tested beyond skill, beyond intelligence, and beyond resources. What remains is the raw question of will: will you continue when the odds are against you. Those who have endured will testify that endurance is not simply an act of stubbornness but a refined posture of resilience built from conviction. It is the refusal to allow temporary conditions to dictate permanent choices. It is the ability to see failure as information rather than identity. It is the courage to rise again when the ground beneath you has collapsed. Entrepreneurs who understand this principle recognize that the world does not reward those who start well but those who finish, and finishing requires staying power. History offers countless lessons of endurance as the deciding factor between obscurity and greatness. Thomas Edison did not invent the light bulb on his first attempt. He failed thousands of times, yet in his own words he had not failed but discovered thousands of ways that would not work. His success was not because he was the only one capable of invention but because he chose not to quit. The Wright brothers endured ridicule and financial struggle, yet their persistence gave humanity the gift of flight. These stories remind us that the foundation of endurance is universal and timeless. It applies whether you are building a global enterprise or nurturing a small business in a local community. The context may differ but the requirement remains the same: when obstacles arise, will you stand or will you flee. Building this foundation begins with clarity of purpose. Entrepreneurs who lack clarity are easily discouraged, for without a clear reason to endure every difficulty appears unnecessary. The one who is driven only by profit will give up when profits delay. The one who is driven only by recognition will retreat when applause is withheld. But the one who is driven by a deep purpose, a sense that their work is tied to impact beyond themselves, will endure even when evidence of success is scarce. Purpose creates an inner reservoir of energy that sustains entrepreneurs when outer resources have dried up. When you know why you started, you are less likely to abandon the journey midway. Endurance therefore is not accidental; it is cultivated by anchoring yourself to a vision larger than present struggles. Another element of this foundation is discipline. Endurance is not only about surviving crises but about consistently showing up when nothing seems urgent. Discipline creates habits, and habits sustain endurance. The business leader who practices financial discipline, who avoids unnecessary debts, who saves for lean times, will endure storms that wipe out others. The entrepreneur who disciplines their mind, who refuses to indulge in self-pity or destructive comparison, will find strength to move forward while others are paralyzed. Discipline is what allows entrepreneurs to continue the slow, daily tasks that build momentum, even when excitement has faded. Without discipline, passion burns quickly and leaves nothing but ashes. With discipline, even small efforts accumulate into endurance. The foundation of endurance is also built through adaptability. Many entrepreneurs quit not because they lacked determination but because they lacked flexibility. To endure does not mean to resist change; it means to survive by embracing it. The market will evolve, technologies will advance, and consumer expectations will shift. Endurance requires the humility to adapt while remaining faithful to core values. Businesses that endure for generations are those that reinvent themselves without losing their identity. The entrepreneur who insists on repeating yesterday's methods in today's environment is choosing extinction over endurance. Adaptability ensures that the entrepreneur's commitment is not to a specific tactic but to the larger vision. In this way, endurance becomes not the blind repetition of the past but the intelligent persistence of purpose across changing seasons. Yet perhaps the most hidden part of this foundation is emotional resilience. Entrepreneurship exposes the individual to constant rejection, criticism, and pressure. Without emotional resilience, even the strongest plans collapse under the weight of discouragement. Endurance requires the ability to manage fear without being paralyzed, to handle failure without being defined by it, and to accept criticism without losing confidence. Emotional resilience is not natural to all, but it can be cultivated. It grows when one learns to separate self-worth from immediate results, when one seeks counsel and community instead of isolation, and when one maintains hope even when circumstances look bleak. The entrepreneur who can regulate emotions in times of crisis has already built half the foundation of endurance. It is important to note that endurance is not passive waiting but active persistence. It is not about sitting in failure hoping for a miracle but about continuing to work, to try, and to adjust. Some confuse endurance with inactivity, but true endurance is relentless forward motion, even if slow, even if painful, even if invisible to others. Every step, no matter how small, is a declaration that quitting is not an option. Endurance is measured not in dramatic victories but in the daily refusal to give up. It is in the business owner who opens their shop every morning despite yesterday's losses, in the founder who keeps pitching their idea despite a hundred rejections, in the innovator who continues to refine their product though investors have turned away. These are the silent acts of endurance that eventually blossom into visible success. The foundation of endurance also has a communal dimension. No entrepreneur truly endures alone. Support networks, mentors, partners, and even loyal customers contribute to the sustaining power of a business. Wise entrepreneurs understand that endurance is amplified when shared. They cultivate relationships that encourage persistence, they surround themselves with people who believe in their vision, and they lean on others when their own strength falters. To endure without community is to carry a burden heavier than necessary. The foundation therefore is not only individual resolve but also collective reinforcement. Finally, building the foundation of endurance requires a mindset that views time differently. Entrepreneurs who expect instant results are often the first to quit. Endurance is built on the recognition that meaningful growth takes time. Just as seeds require seasons to become trees, businesses require patience to mature. The entrepreneur who accepts this truth will endure the waiting without frustration, will interpret delays as natural, and will keep watering the vision until it bears fruit. Impatience destroys endurance, but those who master patience discover that time is not their enemy but their ally. In conclusion, the foundation of endurance is not glamorous but it is indispensable. It is made of purpose, discipline, adaptability, emotional resilience, active persistence, community, and patience. Entrepreneurs who cultivate this foundation create businesses that can weather storms, outlast trends, and remain relevant when others have disappeared. When others quit, the enduring entrepreneur stands. When others surrender, the enduring entrepreneur tries again. When others count losses, the enduring entrepreneur prepares for the next gain. This is the essence of building the foundation of endurance, and without it, no business can truly thrive.

The Test of Commitment

Endurance cannot be spoken of without addressing the test of commitment, for commitment is the true evidence of what we are willing to stand by when comfort is no longer guaranteed. Every entrepreneur begins with excitement, with ideas fresh and visions grand, yet as soon as challenges arise, the test begins. This test is not theoretical; it shows up in the very real form of bills that cannot be paid, clients who walk away, deals that collapse at the last minute, employees who lose faith, and family members who begin to question why the struggle is worth it. At that point the dreamer is separated from the doer, and the one who endures is separated from the one who abandons the pursuit. Commitment is not demonstrated when all is well; it is revealed in the darkest hours when everything inside argues that quitting is reasonable. Businesses collapse not simply because the model failed but because the entrepreneur failed the test of commitment. The test of commitment begins with the choice to remain focused on the original vision even when short term results seem invisible. The marketplace is filled with temptations, distractions, and opportunities that appear to offer faster relief. A struggling entrepreneur may be tempted to abandon the long term project to chase quick gains, yet in doing so they lose the integrity of their purpose. Commitment is the voice that says, I will stay on course even if it takes longer, even if it costs more, even if it isolates me, because I know that my vision is worth it. This is what separates leaders who create enduring businesses from those who leave behind unfinished attempts. Endurance is not simply the refusal to quit but the willingness to recommit every single day when the temptation to give up resurfaces. In this way commitment is not a one-time decision but a continuous reaffirmation of resolve. The test of commitment also involves the ability to keep investing when returns are delayed. It is easy to invest money, energy, and time when profits come quickly. The real test is whether you will continue pouring yourself into the work when nothing comes back immediately. Many businesses collapse in their infancy because the founders expect returns faster than the process allows. Enduring entrepreneurs understand that commitment means sowing without always seeing immediate harvest. They understand that every effort, even when invisible, accumulates. Commitment therefore is not blind hope but trust in the unseen work beneath the surface. Just as seeds germinate quietly in the soil long before they break the ground, businesses develop in unseen ways long before profits become visible. Entrepreneurs who endure this waiting season show the strength of their commitment.

The test of commitment further reveals itself in the sacrifices required along the way. Commitment often demands letting go of comfort, sleep, leisure, and sometimes even the approval of others. Friends may not understand why you keep pursuing an idea that has not yet produced results. Family may question your decisions when financial strain increases. Society may judge you as unrealistic or stubborn. Yet true commitment is not swayed by external approval. It is anchored in conviction rather than applause. Those who endure learn to walk through loneliness without abandoning their path. They learn to trust the worth of their vision even when others mock it. This willingness to sacrifice immediate comfort for long term impact is one of the clearest signs of genuine commitment. At the heart of this test is the discipline of consistency. Commitment without consistency is only an intention, but consistency transforms commitment into reality. The entrepreneur who keeps showing up, who keeps refining the product, who keeps serving the customer, even when results are slow, proves their endurance. Many give up too soon because they expect success to be an event rather than a process. Enduring entrepreneurs recognize that success is a gradual accumulation of consistent effort. They may not win every day, but they show up every day. They may not close a deal in every meeting, but they attend every meeting prepared. They may not always be motivated, but they discipline themselves to act regardless of mood. This is commitment in its purest form: to continue doing what must be done, not because it feels rewarding, but because it is necessary for the vision to survive. The test of commitment also comes in the form of resilience against discouragement. Criticism will come, and often it will come from those whose voices carry weight in our lives. Potential investors may dismiss an idea as unviable. Friends may advise pursuing something easier. Colleagues may laugh at failed attempts. Competitors may celebrate your setbacks. In such moments, commitment is tested by whether you allow the voices of discouragement to silence your own belief. Endurance demands that you remain committed even when respected voices disagree. This does not mean ignoring wise counsel but it does mean distinguishing between caution and defeatism. Commitment chooses to listen, adapt if necessary, but never surrender to hopelessness. It is also important to acknowledge that the test of commitment is not passed in grand gestures but in small daily choices. An entrepreneur may endure a major setback and find the strength to continue, yet the real test is in the countless smaller moments where quitting feels convenient. It is in waking up one more morning to face rejection again, in making one more phone call to a potential client, in sending one more proposal after ten have been ignored. These small decisions accumulate into the weight of commitment. They are rarely celebrated, but they form the backbone of endurance. Businesses do not collapse overnight; they collapse through repeated small decisions to stop trying. Likewise, businesses do not succeed overnight; they succeed through repeated small decisions to keep trying. The test of commitment therefore is a daily examination, not an occasional one. Commitment is also tested by failure itself. When an idea collapses or a plan backfires, some interpret it as the end. Yet enduring entrepreneurs interpret failure as data, as a tool for refinement. They commit not to a single tactic but to the larger vision. This means that even when one attempt fails, they remain committed to finding another way. Failure does not dislodge them from their path; it simply redirects their steps. In this way, commitment becomes flexible without losing its strength. Those who lack commitment interpret failure as proof that they should quit. Those who possess commitment interpret failure as proof that they must try again differently. This difference in interpretation is often the dividing line between those who endure and those who surrender.

Perhaps the most profound test of commitment is whether the entrepreneur is willing to persist when recognition is absent. Many dreams of success for the applause it brings, yet the journey requires long seasons of obscurity. For months or even years, no one may notice your efforts. The world may pass by without acknowledgment of your sacrifices. In such times, commitment means working for the vision rather than the visibility. It means building in silence, trusting that in due time the results will speak. Those who endure learn to detach their motivation from recognition. They understand that the greatest work often grows in hiddenness before it is revealed. This ability to remain committed to obscurity separates those who thrive long term from those who vanish quickly. The test of commitment is not designed to destroy but to refine. It is through these tests that entrepreneurs grow the muscles required to sustain success. If success were given without tests, it would collapse under the weight of unpreparedness. Commitment is therefore not only about survival but about preparation. Each test strengthens character, sharpens focus, and increases capacity. Entrepreneurs who endure these tests emerge not only with thriving businesses but with transformed character. They become leaders capable of carrying the weight of responsibility that enduring success demands. In this sense, the test of commitment is a gift disguised as struggle. It molds entrepreneurs into individuals who can handle success without being destroyed by it. In conclusion, the test of commitment is the unavoidable path every entrepreneur must walk. It demands patience when results are slow, sacrifice when comfort is tempting, consistency when motivation is absent, resilience when criticism is loud, courage when failure is fresh, and humility when recognition is withheld. Endurance is proven not in words but in the passing of this test. Those who remain committed despite the weight of challenges build businesses that stand when others crumble. The test will always come, but the outcome depends on the choice made: to quit or to endure. And in this choice lies the destiny of every entrepreneur who seeks to thrive when others have surrendered.

The Reward of Persistence

The reward of persistence is not always immediate but it is inevitable for those who truly endure, and this truth forms the ultimate encouragement for entrepreneurs who commit to stand firm when every circumstance tells them to quit. Persistence is the continuous decision to keep moving forward despite obstacles, to hold on to vision when evidence is scarce, to keep planting seeds even when harvest has not appeared, and to refuse surrender when the pain of the journey becomes overwhelming. It is persistence that transforms dreams into realities and separates those who admire success from those who achieve it. Every great business story we celebrate today is in essence a story of persistence that refused to bow to difficulty. When we speak of reward it is easy to think only of financial profit, but the true reward of persistence is far greater. It includes the maturity of character, the strength of resilience, the credibility earned in the eyes of others, and the inner satisfaction of knowing you did not abandon your purpose. Money comes and goes, markets rise and fall, but the legacy of persistence is a reward that outlasts financial cycles. An entrepreneur who has persisted through storms gains the unshakable confidence that no crisis can destroy them. This confidence itself becomes an asset greater than any product they sell. Customers, investors, and even competitors recognize the power of persistence, for it communicates reliability. When people see that you do not abandon your vision in times of difficulty, they begin to trust that your business can be relied upon. Trust is the most valuable currency in any market, and persistence is the price that earns it. Businesses that quit too early communicate instability and discourage long term partners, but those that endure even when small, even when struggling, build a reputation that becomes a reward in itself. Another reward of persistence is the compounding effect of effort. Each small action that feels insignificant at the moment accumulates over time. The entrepreneur who continues to show up daily, who continues to refine their craft, who continues to pursue clients, eventually discovers that persistence multiplies results. At first progress may be invisible, but persistence ensures that the invisible eventually becomes visible. Seeds sown day after day, watered by consistency, grow roots beneath the soil until suddenly a tree emerges. To the outsider it looks like an overnight success, but to the entrepreneur it is the delayed reward of long persistence. The world celebrates the fruit without always acknowledging the years of persistence that produced it. Those who quit never experience this compounding effect because they stop just before results begin to appear. Persistence is the bridge between effort and reward, and only those who cross it see the outcome. The reward of persistence is also found in the development of resilience that spreads beyond business into every area of life. Entrepreneurs who have persisted through failure, through loss, and through rejection emerge with a strength that cannot be faked. They become more patient in relationships, more courageous in decisions, more hopeful in uncertainties. Persistence molds character in ways that success without struggle never can. This transformation is often the most valuable reward because businesses may rise and fall but the resilient character built through persistence remains. It becomes a resource that can be applied to new ventures, to community leadership, and even to personal challenges outside of business. Persistence therefore rewards not only with external success but with internal transformation. Another dimension of the reward is the ability to inspire others. When an entrepreneur persists and finally breaks through, their story becomes a source of motivation for countless others who are on the edge of quitting. Persistence creates testimonies that ripple across generations. A single life of endurance can ignite hope in many who believe their struggle is unique. This is why the reward of persistence cannot be measured only in personal gain. It extends to the influence you have on others, to the lives encouraged by your refusal to give up. A community strengthened by your story is a reward greater than any financial success. People begin to see not only your product but your persistence as a symbol of what is possible. The reward of persistence is also the authority it gives you in your field. When you have persisted through years of practice and learning, you acquire a depth of knowledge that newcomers cannot replicate. This authority makes your voice respected, your expertise sought after, and your leadership trusted. It opens doors that are close to those who gave up early. Many entrepreneurs dream of influence and recognition, but they forget that the price is persistence. Authority cannot be bought; it is earned by the credibility of enduring when others have vanished. This is why the most respected figures in business are not those who had quick flashes of success but those who remained relevant over decades. Their persistence became their qualification, and their reward is the enduring influence they hold. Persistence also carries the reward of unexpected opportunities. When you remain in the game long enough, doors you never imagined begin to open. Investors who once ignored you begin to notice. Collaborations that once seemed impossible become available. Customers who once rejected you return with interest. These rewards do not appear to those who have quit because opportunity visits those who are still present. Persistence ensures that when the door opens, you are there to walk through it. Too many entrepreneurs quit just before their breakthrough, leaving their reward unclaimed. The hidden truth is that many rewards of persistence are time sensitive; they appear only after prolonged endurance, and only those who wait discover them. Financial reward, of course, is also part of persistence, for eventually consistent effort attracts revenue. A business that continues to serve, continues to improve, continues to market, eventually captures loyal customers. Revenue may be delayed but persistence ensures it accumulates. The financial reward is often greater for those who endure because the market trusts longevity. People invest more in businesses that have survived storms than in those that appeared yesterday. Persistence therefore not only brings profit but multiplies it over time. Yet even greater than financial reward is the peace of fulfillment. There is a satisfaction that comes from knowing you did not abandon your vision. This inner peace cannot be purchased; it is earned only through persistence. It is the quiet joy of looking back and realizing that every sacrifice was worth it, that every rejection was part of the journey, that every tear was a seed for the harvest you now enjoy. This fulfillment is a reward that endures long after money has been spent. It remains in your heart as evidence that you lived with courage and refused to surrender. The reward of persistence also teaches others the value of patience. In a generation obsessed with speed, your story becomes a countercultural lesson that good things take time. Your life becomes a living message to others that endurance is not outdated but essential. This teaching effect is itself a reward because it positions you as a mentor, a guide, and a model for future entrepreneurs. Your persistence shapes the culture around you, creating a ripple effect of endurance in those who follow. In conclusion, the reward of persistence is multifaceted. It produces trust in the marketplace, compounding results, resilient character, inspirational stories, lasting authority, unexpected opportunities, financial stability, inner fulfillment, and cultural influence. None of these rewards are granted to those who quit early. They belong exclusively to those who endure. Persistence is never wasted; every act of holding on, every decision to try again, every refusal to quit, becomes an investment that guarantees eventual reward. The only question is whether the entrepreneur will stay long enough to see it. Those who persist discover that success is not a single moment but a continuous unfolding of rewards that increase with time. This is why persistence is not only a survival tactic but a strategy of greatness. The entrepreneur who persists does not merely thrive when others quit; they rise to levels others will never reach because they chose to remain in the journey until the reward appeared, and once the reward appears it justifies every sacrifice made along the way.

2

The Trials That Shape Endurance

In business the difference between those who fade away and those who stand the test of time is often not found in brilliance nor in sudden strokes of luck but in the trials that shape endurance because every entrepreneur will encounter moments when the easy choice is to walk away and every enterprise will pass through storms that threaten its very survival yet it is in these moments that the essence of endurance is carved into the heart of the entrepreneur and into the culture of the business itself for when we speak of trials we are not merely talking about temporary inconveniences but about the difficult seasons when cash flow dries up when employees lose faith when investors withdraw when competitors launch relentless attacks and when the market shifts with no warning leaving even the most carefully designed strategies looking obsolete and useless and yet it is precisely within these experiences that an entrepreneur discovers whether he or she possesses the resilience to adapt, to hold on, and to push forward when everything seems to be falling apart because endurance is not a theoretical trait but a practical force forged in adversity and proven only in the face of obstacles that appear impossible to overcome and this is why those who thrive in business when others quit are never those who avoided trials but those who walked through them and came out stronger than before because endurance cannot be cultivated in comfort and ease it must be formed in the crucible of setbacks rejections failures and disappointments that test the will to continue and it is here that a business leader must decide whether to surrender to despair or to rise with renewed determination. The trials that shape endurance are often lonely and brutal and they rarely arrive when convenient for they come when resources are thin and energy is drained and confidence is shaken and when the entrepreneur feels most vulnerable yet they demand from the leader an unshakable resolve to remain standing when everything inside whispers that the fight is no longer worth it and this is where the stories of enduring businesses differ from those that vanish because those who endure do not measure progress by the absence of pain but by the ability to keep advancing despite the pain they do not expect a smooth path but learn to dance on rough ground they do not wait for perfect timing but create opportunities in imperfect conditions and they do not view trials as punishment but as preparation for a bigger future because every test faced and survived adds another layer of strength to the foundation of endurance and this foundation cannot be shaken easily by future storms since each trial builds a memory of resilience that becomes a source of courage for the next challenge. When we examine the lives of entrepreneurs who thrived when others quit we find that they were marked not by uninterrupted success but by their persistence in the midst of repeated challenges and failures and when those around them surrendered they pressed forward with clarity and courage because endurance taught them to see beyond temporary obstacles to the larger vision and this vision became the anchor that sustained them during difficult seasons and without such endurance even the most brilliant idea can be crushed by the weight of trials since talent without persistence rarely survives the pressure of business reality but persistence even without extraordinary talent often triumphs because it refuses to die when adversity strikes and this is the truth that separates endurance-driven leaders from those who quit too soon. The trials that shape endurance are also teachers because they reveal hidden weaknesses expose false assumptions strip away illusions and force the entrepreneur to confront limitations and blind spots and while the lessons may be painful they prepare the entrepreneur to build with greater wisdom going forward because a leader who has been tested by trials emerges with humility sharpened intuition and the discipline to avoid shortcuts for shortcuts may promise ease but they rob the business of depth and stability while endurance forces the leader to build systems that can survive long-term pressures and this is why the businesses that stand for decades are almost always those whose founders endured painful trials in the early years because those trials forced them to adopt practices of excellence discipline and innovation that later became the pillars of sustained success. Another important aspect of the trials that shape endurance is that they separate those who are driven by fleeting interest from those who are driven by conviction because interest is fragile and collapses under pressure but conviction grows stronger with opposition and only those who are deeply convicted about their mission their product or their purpose will endure through long seasons of difficulty because they have something inside them that refuses to let go even when external conditions scream that it is time to stop and that is why enduring entrepreneurs are never only motivated by profit they are sustained by vision by belief in what they are creating and by a sense of responsibility to bring their contribution into reality and when profit disappears temporarily they keep going because they see beyond short-term gain into long-term impact and this mindset transforms trials from discouragement into fuel for perseverance. Endurance also requires a redefinition of success in the midst of trials because many entrepreneurs quit simply because they measure success wrongly and when the immediate results fail to meet their expectations they assume failure has won yet endurance-driven leaders understand that survival itself in the midst of trials is success because if they can remain standing today there will be another chance tomorrow to move forward and it is this ability to stay alive in the fight when others are leaving the battlefield that eventually creates the opportunity for breakthrough and it is often after the most intense trials that the greatest victories come because trials have a way of clearing the path of those who lack conviction leaving only those who are ready to pay the price of true achievement and when that moment of opportunity arrives it is the enduring leader who remains to seize it while others who quit earlier are left regretting the decision to abandon their path. The shaping of endurance through trials also has a contagious effect on the culture of the business because when employees see a leader who refuses to surrender they learn to adopt the same resilience and when partners see consistency in the face of difficulty their trust deepens and when customers observe a brand that continues to deliver value despite setbacks their loyalty grows stronger and in this way the trials faced by a leader not only strengthen the individual but also strengthen the entire organization creating a culture of persistence that cannot be easily broken and this cultural endurance becomes a competitive advantage in markets where many businesses collapse at the first sign of trouble. Finally the trials that shape endurance must not be viewed as unfortunate interruptions but as necessary seasons for without them endurance would remain untested and unproven and no leader can claim true resilience without passing through hardship because the capacity to endure is like a muscle it grows only through resistance and pressure and those who avoid resistance remain weak while those who embrace it gain strength and therefore every entrepreneur who aspires to thrive in business when others quit must embrace the reality that trials are not to be feared but to be faced with courage because it is through these trials that the endurance factor is developed and it is this endurance factor that ultimately separates those who merely start businesses from those who build legacies that last long after others have quit.

The Mental Fortitude Behind Perseverance

In business every obstacle encountered is first confronted in the mind long before it is tackled in reality and this is why the endurance factor relies heavily on mental fortitude because while physical resources financial backing and skilled teams play important roles in the survival of a business it is the strength of the mind of the entrepreneur that ultimately decides whether the journey continues or collapses under pressure and when we speak of mental fortitude we are referring to the ability to remain focused calm and determined when faced with chaos uncertainty and fear for without this quality even the strongest vision will wither in the face of discouragement since the human mind is the battlefield where either endurance wins or surrender takes over and this is why cultivating mental strength is indispensable for anyone who wants to thrive in business when others quit because success is less about what happens to you and more about how you interpret and respond to what happens to you and those responses are born from the depth of mental resilience that you have trained within yourself and this training is not accomplished overnight it is the product of consistent discipline intentional thought patterns and the willingness to reject defeatist beliefs no matter how persuasive circumstances may appear. Mental fortitude begins with clarity of vision because without clarity the mind will easily drift into confusion when trials arise and many entrepreneurs fail not because they lacked resources but because they lost sight of their purpose in the midst of hardship and when vision becomes blurred endurance weakens because the mind has no anchor to hold on to when waves of uncertainty crash and this is why enduring entrepreneurs revisit their vision repeatedly reminding themselves of why they started and where they are going because a clear vision strengthens the mind to press on when nothing seems to be working and it gives meaning to the sacrifices required for perseverance and when meaning is attached to suffering the mind is more likely to endure it but when there is no meaning the pain feels pointless and unbearable leading to surrender and collapse. Mental fortitude also involves mastery over fear because fear is the most common weapon that trials use to paralyze entrepreneurs it whispers that failure is inevitable it amplifies every setback it magnifies every risk and it convinces the leader that quitting is the most rational choice yet those with strong mental endurance learn not to deny fear but to confront it and reframe it as a signal for growth rather than destruction and they recognize that fear is often an exaggeration of reality a projection of worst case scenarios that rarely manifest and by challenging fear with facts with confidence and with unshakable belief in their mission they strip it of its power and transform it into fuel for bolder action and when fear loses its grip the mind becomes free to persist regardless of uncertainty. Another dimension of mental fortitude is emotional regulation because entrepreneurship is filled with emotional highs and lows moments of elation when victories are won and moments of despair when losses pile up and if a leader is tossed violently by every emotion endurance cannot survive because the mind will burn out from instability but those who thrive in difficult times develop the discipline to remain steady whether in success or failure they do not allow arrogance to cloud judgment in seasons of prosperity nor do they allow despair to cripple them in seasons of loss instead they cultivate emotional balance which enables rational decision making and preserves energy for the long run and this balance is not the absence of feeling but the mastery of feeling where emotions serve the leader instead of control the leader and this emotional stability is a crucial component of mental strength because it creates consistency which is the heartbeat of endurance. Discipline of thought is another hallmark of mental fortitude because the mind naturally gravitates toward doubt negativity and distraction especially when difficulties arise and unless it is trained it will surrender to these impulses and sabotage endurance but entrepreneurs who thrive when others quit discipline their thinking through intentional focus affirmations of belief and continuous learning they guard against toxic voices that plant seeds of hopelessness they filter information so that their minds are nourished with clarity and solutions instead of fear and confusion and they practice mental habits that keep them aligned with their long term mission and this disciplined mind becomes a fortress that protects endurance when external forces try to dismantle it because while circumstances may be beyond control the mind remains within control and mastery of it ensures that the leader stands firm when others crumble. Another aspect of mental fortitude is adaptability because rigidity in thought often leads to frustration when reality fails to conform to expectations but endurance thrives in flexible minds that can adjust strategies without abandoning vision they can pivot when necessary without seeing the pivot as defeat they can accept temporary detours without losing sight of the destination and this adaptability keeps the entrepreneur moving forward when others give up in frustration and it creates innovative solutions that transform setbacks into stepping stones because the mind that adapts refuses to see failure as final but views it instead as feedback for improvement and this mental shift makes perseverance not only possible but productive since each obstacle becomes a lesson rather than a dead end. Mental endurance also requires an inner narrative of resilience because the stories we tell ourselves in the midst of adversity determine whether we continue or collapse and those who quit often feed themselves narratives of inadequacy and hopelessness convincing themselves that they are not good enough or that their journey is cursed to fail but those with strong mental fortitude tell themselves stories of strength persistence and eventual triumph they remind themselves of past victories they declare that challenges are temporary and they frame their struggles as the price of greatness and these narratives fuel their spirit to keep moving when the body is exhausted and the environment is hostile and by constantly reinforcing this inner dialogue of resilience they build an internal atmosphere where endurance thrives naturally because belief fuels action and action fuels progress. Another dimension of mental strength is patience because endurance in business is not only about the capacity to withstand pain but also about the willingness to wait for results and impatience has destroyed more businesses than outright failure because entrepreneurs who demand instant success are easily discouraged when outcomes are delayed yet those with mental fortitude understand that great achievements require time to mature and they accept the reality that seasons of planting do not immediately produce harvests but they continue watering and cultivating with faith that the reward will come and this patience sustains endurance because it prevents premature surrender and it transforms waiting seasons into working seasons where unseen progress is taking place beneath the surface preparing for eventual breakthrough. To sustain mental fortitude an entrepreneur must also embrace solitude because the mind is strengthened in reflection and silence where clarity emerges away from the noise of constant demands and enduring leaders carve out time to renew their thoughts evaluate their journey and reset their focus because without this personal renewal the mind becomes cluttered overwhelmed and eventually fatigued to the point of surrender but solitude restores energy sharpens perspective and refuels the will to persevere and therefore it is a critical discipline for those who want to thrive when others quit. Finally mental fortitude is anchored in hope because without hope the mind will collapse under sustained pressure hope is the light that keeps the entrepreneur moving through the darkest tunnel it is the belief that tomorrow can be better than today it is the assurance that every trial has an end and that persistence will not be wasted and when hope is alive endurance becomes natural because the mind can envision a future worth suffering for and that vision gives strength to endure what others cannot and this is why cultivating hope through faith through inspiring environments through uplifting relationships and through constant reminders of purpose is essential for every entrepreneur who wants to thrive when others quit because no matter how fierce the battle may become a mind anchored in hope can never be fully defeated and it will carry the entrepreneur through storms into seasons of triumph that justify every sacrifice made along the way.

Turning Pain into Power

In business no leader escapes pain because pain is woven into the very fabric of entrepreneurship it arrives through failures that sting through betrayals that wound through financial losses that paralyze and through long nights of uncertainty that weigh heavily on the spirit yet what separates those who thrive when others quit is not the absence of pain but the way they respond to it and this is where the endurance factor shines most brightly because those who endure have learned to turn pain into power rather than allowing it to become poison they use it as fuel for growth as a source of clarity and as a teacher that refines both character and strategy and when we study the lives of entrepreneurs who achieved lasting success their journeys are never stories of uninterrupted joy but stories of pain transformed into strength setbacks converted into wisdom and heartbreak reimagined as resilience and it is this ability to reinterpret pain that ensures survival in moments when others surrender because while quitting may seem like the easiest way to escape discomfort enduring leaders choose instead to embrace it harness it and channel it toward building businesses that become stronger precisely because of the struggles they endured. Pain is inevitable but suffering is a choice and those who thrive in business understand this difference because while they cannot prevent painful experiences they can decide whether to allow that pain to consume them or to convert it into something useful and enduring leaders always choose conversion they let disappointment sharpen their determination they let failure ignite creativity and they let rejection build unshakable confidence for every painful experience carries within it the potential for transformation and those who endure understand how to extract that potential while those who quit see only the wound and miss the lesson and by refusing to let pain define them enduring entrepreneurs define pain itself as a stepping stone toward greatness and this mindset keeps them advancing when others collapse under the weight of frustration. One of the most powerful ways to turn pain into power is by allowing it to expand perspective because pain has a way of forcing reflection it makes leaders ask deeper questions about purpose about strategy and about resilience and in this reflection lies the opportunity to discover truths that comfort would have kept hidden and these truths often lead to breakthroughs that reshape the trajectory of a business because a leader who has been tested by pain emerges wiser more humble and more capable of navigating complex realities and without pain many entrepreneurs remain shallow chasing only quick wins but pain forces them to consider depth sustainability and long term impact and it strengthens their ability to make decisions that will stand the test of time and this expanded perspective becomes a source of power because it prevents repeated mistakes and equips the leader to handle future storms with greater ease. Another way that pain becomes power is through the discipline it enforces because painful experiences strip away illusions of ease and entitlement and they teach leaders the necessity of consistency and sacrifice they eliminate the belief that success comes without cost and they engrain habits of persistence that cannot be developed in comfort and this discipline is what separates businesses that endure from those that crumble because without discipline even the greatest resources will be squandered but with discipline even limited resources can be multiplied into lasting success and when pain teaches discipline it leaves behind a gift that continues to serve the entrepreneur long after the wound has healed for the habits born in struggle become the foundation for future triumphs. Pain also has a unique way of building empathy and empathy is a powerful currency in business because leaders who have suffered understand the struggles of employees customers and partners in a deeper way they lead with compassion they design products with genuine concern for user needs and they build cultures that value humanity alongside profit and this empathy creates trust and loyalty which are essential for long term success and so the pain that once seemed destructive becomes a source of connection that binds a business to its stakeholders in ways that competitors cannot easily replicate and this connection becomes power because loyalty cannot be bought it must be earned and it is most deeply earned by leaders who have been through pain and emerged with hearts that care more for people than for short term profit. Enduring leaders also turn pain into power by letting it fuel innovation because nothing forces creativity like crisis and when the pain of loss or failure strikes it pushes the mind to think beyond old patterns and to search desperately for new solutions and many of the world's greatest innovations were born not in times of comfort but in moments of intense pain when survival demanded reinvention and this is why enduring entrepreneurs embrace painful seasons not as the end but as the birthplace of reinvention and by refusing to quit in these moments they discover creative paths that others never find because they left the race too soon and this creativity becomes power because it positions the business uniquely in the marketplace offering solutions forged in fire that others cannot easily duplicate. Another transformation that pain brings is resilience because every time an entrepreneur endures pain and survives it they develop a deeper belief in their capacity to withstand future challenges and this resilience compounds over time until it becomes unshakable confidence and when a leader knows from experience that they can endure loss rejection or failure they no longer fear these possibilities and this absence of fear makes them bolder in their decisions willing to take risks that others avoid and this boldness often leads to breakthroughs because progress in business is reserved for those willing to take calculated risks and when pain has stripped away the paralyzing fear of failure the entrepreneur gains freedom to act with courage and vision and this freedom is a form of power that pain uniquely delivers. Pain also refines purpose because in the midst of comfort it is easy to drift into distractions but pain forces the entrepreneur to ask why am I still doing this why is this worth enduring and in answering these questions the leader reconnects with the deeper purpose that originally inspired the journey and this clarity of purpose reignites passion and gives new energy to persevere and when purpose is clarified through pain it becomes a source of unstoppable drive because the entrepreneur now knows not only what they are doing but why they are doing it and that why becomes the fuel that keeps the fire burning even in the darkest hours and this is another way that pain becomes power by cutting away the superficial and leaving only what truly matters. A further strength that pain creates is credibility because in business words are cheap and promises are many but credibility is built when leaders demonstrate through lived experience that they can endure hardship and remain faithful to their mission and people trust those who have scars because scars prove survival scars tell stories of endurance and scars communicate that this leader has faced the worst and is still standing and that credibility becomes power because employees will follow a scarred but standing leader customers will trust a scarred but surviving brand and investors will believe in a scarred but resilient entrepreneur far more than in someone who has never been tested and thus the very pain that once seemed like it would destroy the business becomes the badge that legitimizes it in the eyes of the world. Finally pain becomes power when it is used as testimony to inspire others because endurance is not only for personal survival it is also for collective encouragement and when entrepreneurs share how they endured pain and still triumphed they give hope to others who are ready to quit and in this way pain becomes multiplied power because it not only strengthens the one who experienced it but also empowers countless others to continue and this ripple effect transforms individual endurance into a legacy of resilience that shapes entire communities of entrepreneurs who refuse to quit and so the pain endured by one becomes the fuel for perseverance in many and this is one of the greatest gifts pain can give turning personal struggle into communal strength and ensuring that no endurance is ever wasted. Therefore the key to thriving in business when others quit is not avoiding pain but learning to transform it for every entrepreneur will encounter pain but not every entrepreneur will know how to harness it and those who quit are those who see pain only as an enemy while those who endure are those who see pain as a secret ally an uninvited but powerful teacher and once embraced this teacher reveals that every wound can become wisdom every scar can become strength and every tear can become testimony and when this transformation takes place pain no longer controls the entrepreneur the entrepreneur controls pain and channels it into power and this is the essence of endurance the ability to turn what was meant to break you into the very thing that builds you and it is this transformation that ensures survival growth and triumph when others have already surrendered.

3

Seeing Beyond the Immediate Struggles

The real difference between those who quit and those who thrive often comes down to one single quality which is vision and not just the vision of a nice dream but a long term vision that guides decisions when the present is unbearable and the future looks uncertain. Every entrepreneur faces moments where it feels like all efforts are collapsing and where every logical reason suggests it is time to quit yet the ones who rise above do so because they hold a vision that is bigger than the immediate storm. Long term vision gives meaning to the struggle because it shifts attention away from the pain of the present toward the rewards of persistence. It becomes the compass that reminds a business owner why they started and why it matters to keep going. Without vision businesses crumble not because the idea was bad but because the founder could not see past the current challenge. With vision even the toughest storm is framed as a temporary interruption rather than a permanent end. True vision is not just about having a statement on paper or a catchy line on a wall. It is about crafting a clear mental picture of where the business is heading in ten years twenty years or even fifty years and using that picture to endure the darkest of moments. When cash flow dries up and creditors are knocking vision reminds the entrepreneur that this is not the end. When competitors seem stronger and more resourced vision becomes the inner fire that says this business was built for something greater than this temporary setback. Many people make the mistake of confusing vision with goals. Goals are targets that can be achieved or missed but vision is a living belief that shapes identity. Goals may be adjusted but vision rarely changes. For instance if a business goal is to make one million dollars in revenue by the end of the year that is admirable but if the business vision is to redefine how customers experience service in its industry then the vision remains relevant even if the one million dollar goal is missed. This perspective allows the entrepreneur to recover from failures and to continue building because the larger vision was never tied to one event or one milestone. It is also important to understand that vision has to be both inspiring and demanding. A weak vision will not sustain a business through trials. A powerful vision challenges the entrepreneur to rise to a higher standard. It sets the tone for resilience. When Amazon was struggling in its early days Jeff Bezos did not build around quarterly profit expectations but around a vision of becoming the most customer centric company in the world. That vision gave meaning to every sacrifice and allowed the company to endure losses that would have caused others to shut down. This same pattern can be seen in every enduring business because vision does not collapse when the numbers dip. Instead it fuels decisions that protect the long game. For entrepreneurs who are building environments where challenges are multiplied by limited resources or hostile markets vision becomes even more vital because it prevents distraction. Without vision a business can chase short term opportunities that appear attractive but lead to long term ruin. With vision every decision is tested against the bigger picture and if the decision does not fit the long term design it is rejected no matter how appealing it looks in the present. This discipline builds endurance because it means the entrepreneur is not swayed by the noise of immediate gratification. Furthermore vision has a way of attracting people who believe in the same picture. Employees partners and investors are not drawn merely to profit they are drawn to meaning. When a leader communicates vision clearly it becomes contagious and the entire organization gains the strength to persist even when external conditions scream failure. Customers too resonate with vision. They are not loyal to companies because of products alone but because of the story behind the brand. This is why vision led businesses often outlast product led businesses. The product may change but the vision carries continuity.

Building A Legacy Mindset

Long term vision naturally leads to the idea of legacy and endurance is incomplete without legacy because if all the effort of building a business only lasts for the founder's lifetime then endurance has not truly been achieved. A legacy mindset means building with the intention of transferring strength values and continuity to the next generation of leaders and customers. Too many businesses collapse because the founder built only for immediate survival and never considered what would happen beyond their own active presence. A legacy mindset forces different choices. It forces an entrepreneur to prioritize systems over personality because personality fades while systems endure. It forces the entrepreneur to value principles over trends because trends expire while principles carry relevance across time. This is the mindset that creates businesses which thrive long after others have quit. Legacy is not accidental it is intentional. It is crafted by decisions made daily. It is seen in how the business documents its knowledge how it trains its people how it builds culture and how it positions itself in the marketplace. If a business is driven only by what is fashionable today it may gain rapid attention but it will lose relevance quickly. If however it is anchored in timeless principles of value creation service and customer trust it will remain strong across generations. Consider how businesses like Coca Cola have survived over a century through wars recessions and market disruptions. Their endurance comes not merely from having a great drink but from cultivating a mindset of legacy. They never saw themselves as a temporary company but as a long term institution and every decision flowed from that identity. Entrepreneurs today can learn from this by asking not just how my business will make money today but also how will my business remain relevant in fifty years. A legacy mindset also changes how leaders view people. Instead of using employees as tools to achieve short term results they see them as custodians of vision who will carry the brand further than the founder could alone. They invest in people not because it is convenient but because it is essential for continuity. This creates loyalty and stability which in turn strengthens the ability of the business to endure. Building a legacy also means designing the brand story in such a way that customers feel they are part of something larger than a transaction. When customers buy from a legacy driven company they are not just consuming a product they are participating in a heritage. This emotional connection becomes a powerful shield against competition. It is difficult for a competitor to take customers away from a company that has become part of their identity. Endurance thrives here because the brand ceases to be a business alone and becomes a cultural force.

Vision as the Engine of Endurance

Ultimately endurance without vision is impossible because there will always be reasons to quit but vision provides the one reason to keep going that outweighs them all. Every failure every delay every rejection is reframed as part of the journey rather than the end. Vision keeps the entrepreneur grounded in purpose when money is scarce and motivated in abundance when money is plenty. It prevents arrogance in success and despair in failure. Vision is the engine of endurance because it makes every difficulty meaningful and every victory purposeful. Without vision struggles are random and victories are hollow but with vision struggles become preparation and victories become confirmation. The true test of an entrepreneur's vision is not how excited they are at the beginning but how committed they remain when nothing seems to work. This is where endurance shows itself most powerfully because anyone can start with enthusiasm but only visionaries persist with consistency.

4

Mastering the Psychology of Persistence

Endurance in business is not first a matter of strategy or resources but a matter of the mind because the strongest business plan will collapse if the entrepreneur has a weak inner world while an ordinary plan will often succeed when backed by mental strength that refuses to break. The psychology of persistence is the hidden engine of those who thrive when others quit and it explains why two people facing the same obstacles can have completely different outcomes one giving up after the first defeat and the other pressing forward with greater determination. To master persistence an entrepreneur must first learn to reframe challenges because how the mind interprets events shapes whether endurance is possible or impossible. If every delay is interpreted as rejection then quitting will always feel justified but if every delay is interpreted as preparation then quitting will feel premature and even foolish. The human mind is naturally wired to avoid pain and discomfort and business by its nature is filled with both so the untrained mind will constantly whisper reasons to abandon the path yet the trained mind builds new associations that see pain not as danger but as part of the process. This reframing is not blind optimism but disciplined thinking and it is cultivated by daily practice. Each time an obstacle appears the entrepreneur chooses to interpret it as an opportunity to learn or to test their commitment. Over time this becomes instinctive and persistence becomes less of a struggle and more of a reflex. Another critical part of persistence psychology is emotional regulation because endurance cannot thrive in a chaotic emotional state. Fear anxiety anger and doubt all erode persistence by magnifying problems and reducing clarity. An entrepreneur who reacts emotionally to every difficulty will burn out quickly but one who practices emotional regulation will conserve energy for the long journey. This does not mean suppressing emotions but understanding them and directing them. Fear for example can be redirected into preparation. Instead of allowing fear to paralyze action the entrepreneur can use it as motivation to double check strategies and build stronger safeguards. Anger can be redirected into fuel to prove doubters wrong rather than into reckless decisions. Even doubt can be harnessed as a tool for critical thinking because sometimes doubt exposes blind spots that need correction. When emotions are mastered persistence becomes sustainable because the entrepreneur is not constantly derailed by internal storms. Visualization is another tool that strengthens persistence psychology because the mind holds onto what it can see and when the entrepreneur builds a clear inner picture of the future it provides a reason to endure the present. Olympic athletes use visualization to push through excruciating training and entrepreneurs can do the same by visualizing the business they are building in vivid detail. This mental image serves as a reward that can be accessed even when external rewards are delayed. It keeps motivation alive when circumstances try to suffocate it. Alongside visualization there must be self-talk because the words an entrepreneur speaks to themselves determine their ability to continue. Negative self-talk magnifies defeat while positive self-talk builds resilience. Saying repeatedly that the journey is impossible creates internal resistance but affirming daily that challenges are temporary creates momentum. This is not shallow motivation but rewiring the subconscious because the mind believes what it hears consistently and when persistence is rooted in belief the entrepreneur will continue when logic says stop. Beyond these mental practices the psychology of persistence requires identity alignment because people do not endure for long when their actions are disconnected from their identity. If an entrepreneur sees themselves only as someone trying to make money then setbacks will feel like a personal failure but if they see themselves as builder's creators and contributors then setbacks become part of their identity journey. They will endure not because of money alone but because quitting would mean betraying who they are. This is why many of the world's most enduring entrepreneurs often describe their work not as a job but as a calling. They persist because it is who they are and not just what they do. This alignment gives them stamina that others cannot understand. Persistence also requires a long term relationship with discomfort because endurance is impossible without the ability to sit in pain. The entrepreneur must learn to normalize rejection, normalize slow progress, normalize uncertainty and continue working without losing focus. Most people quit because they assume that discomfort is a signal to stop but the persistent entrepreneur redefines discomfort as proof of growth. Every rejection becomes evidence that they are in motion, every delay becomes evidence that they are being refined, every uncertainty becomes evidence that they are on the path less traveled and that alone gives them a competitive edge. To build this psychology the entrepreneur must practice deliberately putting themselves in situations that stretch them because resilience is like a muscle and it grows only when exercised. By consistently choosing difficult paths instead of easy ones they develop endurance capacity that becomes invaluable when real storms come. Without this preparation even small challenges will break them but with it even overwhelming storms become survivable. In this way the psychology of persistence becomes the foundation upon which all business endurance is built because the body will quit if the mind quits but if the mind refuses to quit the body will always find a way forward.

Building Emotional Resilience for the Entrepreneurial Journey

While the psychology of persistence forms the foundation of endurance it is emotional resilience that determines how long an entrepreneur can truly last because persistence is the decision to keep going but resilience is the capacity to bounce back again and again no matter how deep the fall and no matter how many times setbacks strike. Emotional resilience is the difference between those who collapse under the weight of repeated disappointments and those who rise stronger each time they are knocked down. In business the storms are not occasional interruptions but regular features and only those who build inner strength to process these storms without breaking can endure long enough to succeed. Emotional resilience begins with awareness because one cannot manage what one cannot see. Many entrepreneurs fail not because the challenges were too great but because they were unaware of how those challenges were affecting them internally. They denied their exhaustion, ignored their frustrations, pretended that constant rejection did not hurt, and eventually burned out because suppressed emotions always resurface with greater force. The resilient entrepreneur practices awareness by honestly acknowledging their feelings, admitting when they are tired, recognizing when they are discouraged, and confronting when they are fearful. This awareness does not make them weak but gives them the clarity to address their state before it becomes destructive. Once awareness is in place the next layer of resilience is regulation because awareness without management is dangerous. Regulation is the discipline of deciding how to respond to emotions rather than being controlled by them. For example when a business pitch is rejected after months of preparation the natural emotional response might be shame or anger. The unregulated entrepreneur allows that shame to breed insecurity or that anger to result in rash decisions but the resilient entrepreneur regulates the moment. They allow themselves to feel the sting yet they refuse to act on it destructively. They pause reflect and reframe. They might say this rejection is not a verdict on my identity it is feedback on my strategy and I will use it to improve. This ability to regulate creates stability in the storm and stability is the environment where endurance grows. Another dimension of emotional resilience is recovery because no matter how strong one is constant exposure to pressure will drain emotional energy. Enduring entrepreneurs understand the importance of building recovery practices that replenish their emotional reserves. Some find recovery in solitude and reflection others in time with family or exercise or faith but the principle is the same they intentionally withdraw from the battlefield at intervals to refuel. Without this recovery endurance collapses because emotional depletion eventually leads to physical and mental collapse. Recovery is not a luxury it is a survival strategy. The resilient entrepreneur therefore treats rest not as wasted time but as an investment into longevity. Alongside recovery is adaptability because resilience is not merely about standing firm but also about bending without breaking. Markets shift, technologies evolve, customer expectations change, and regulations appear unexpectedly. An entrepreneur who lacks adaptability confuses rigidity with strength and eventually snaps when pressure mounts. A resilient entrepreneur adapts while maintaining core principles. They are willing to change methods while preserving mission, willing to adjust strategies without abandoning vision. This flexibility allows them to survive shocks that destroy less adaptable competitors. They do not waste emotional energy resisting inevitable change but instead redirect that energy into creating solutions. The heart of resilience also lies in meaning because people can endure almost anything if they believe it is meaningful. Emotional resilience is strengthened when an entrepreneur connects daily struggles to a larger purpose. If difficulties are seen as random they feel unbearable but if they are connected to purpose they feel significant. A mother enduring childbirth focuses not on the pain but on the child she is about to hold. In the same way the resilient entrepreneur interprets struggles as part of a mission that is worth every sacrifice. This sense of meaning becomes the shield that deflects despair. Community is another pillar of resilience because isolation magnifies emotional burdens while connection distributes them. Entrepreneurs often fall into the trap of solitary struggle believing they must appear invincible yet resilience is not built on isolation. It is built in healthy networks where burdens can be shared, perspectives can be offered, and encouragement can be received. Even the strongest minds weaken in silence but within supportive communities' resilience multiplies. Therefore entrepreneurs who endure long enough to thrive intentionally cultivate networks of mentors' peers and supporters who provide both challenge and comfort when storms rage. Resilience is also built by practice. It is not a fixed trait but a skill developed through exposure and reflection. Every time an entrepreneur faces difficulty and chooses to rise instead of quitting their resilience grows. Like a muscle resilience strengthens under pressure. The mistake many make is wishing for a smooth path when in reality it is the rough path that builds the strength to endure. Each disappointment becomes training and each rejection becomes conditioning. Over time what once felt unbearable becomes routine and what once looked impossible becomes achievable. The resilient entrepreneur therefore does not despise difficulties but embraces them as growth partners. A profound dimension of emotional resilience is forgiveness because bitterness drains endurance. In business betrayals are inevitable. Partners may cheat, employees may disappoint, customers may slander, and even family may discourage. Holding on to these wounds' poisons emotional energy and poisons endurance. Forgiveness does not mean excusing injustice but releasing it so it does not consume the builder's focus. Resilient entrepreneurs forgive quickly not because others always deserve it but because they themselves cannot afford the burden of carrying it. This freedom preserves clarity and allows them to continue the journey without being trapped by resentment. Resilience also requires courage because fear is constant in entrepreneurship. Fear of failure, fear of rejection, fear of financial ruin, fear of ridicule. Without courage these fears erode persistence. Courage is not the absence of fear but the decision to act in spite of fear. Each courageous act builds resilience because it proves to the entrepreneur that fear can be felt yet not followed. Over time fear loses its control and resilience becomes the natural state. At the core emotional resilience is the ability to maintain hope when logic suggests despair. Hope is the lifeline of endurance because without hope the entrepreneur will have no reason to rise again after falling. Resilient entrepreneurs guard hope fiercely. They feed it with stories of past victories, with testimonies of others who endured, with reminders of how far they have already come. They refuse to let the flame of hope die and because of that refusal they endure beyond expectations. Emotional resilience then is not an optional attribute but the fuel that sustains persistence. It is the quality that ensures the entrepreneur not only survives storms but grows stronger through them. It is the reason some rise higher after failure while others disappear. Those who cultivate resilience discover that endurance is not simply surviving but thriving in the very environment that breaks others.

Cultivating Mental Toughness for Enduring Leadership

Endurance in business demands a special breed of leadership and that leadership cannot survive without mental toughness because while skills, strategies, and opportunities matter it is toughness of mind that determines who lasts when challenges intensify. Mental toughness is not arrogance and it is not stubbornness, it is the disciplined inner strength that allows a leader to make clear decisions under pressure, to hold firm when everyone else doubts, and to keep moving forward when exhaustion and fear demand retreat. It is the state of mind where excuses lose power and responsibility becomes nonnegotiable. For the entrepreneur mental toughness begins with clarity of focus because scattered attention weakens endurance. A tough mind knows how to prioritize the essential over the urgent and to filter distractions that appear important but add no long term value. This focus creates stability because it channels energy into meaningful work rather than wasting it on noise. Without such focus leadership breaks under pressure because too much energy is wasted reacting instead of building. Tough leaders therefore discipline their minds daily to align thoughts and actions with vision, refusing to be swayed by temporary trends or the voices of those who do not understand their journey. Mental toughness also shows itself in discipline. Discipline is the backbone of enduring leadership because tough leaders understand that feelings are unreliable guides and that success cannot depend on mood. They do what is required whether they feel like it or not. They keep promises to themselves and to others, building trust through consistency. This discipline shows how they manage time, how they approach preparation, and how they execute responsibilities. Where others procrastinate they act, where others make excuses they deliver, and where others compromise they hold the line. Discipline creates reliability and reliability sustains endurance because when followers see that the leader does not break under pressure they gain courage to persist as well. Another dimension of toughness is decisiveness because indecision drains energy and weakens confidence. Tough leaders gather facts, listen to counsel, weigh risks, and then act. They accept that not every decision will be perfect but they refuse to be paralyzed by fear of failure. By acting decisively they keep momentum alive and momentum itself generates endurance. In contrast indecision stalls progress and invites doubt which often destroys a venture before external challenges even arrive. Tough leaders know that mistakes can be corrected but hesitation can be fatal. Mental toughness also requires emotional detachment from constant approval. Many entrepreneurs quit because they crave affirmation and crumble when criticized or ignored. A tough leader learns early that leadership is lonely and that not everyone will celebrate their path. They train their mind to value purpose above popularity. This does not mean ignoring feedback but filtering it, taking what is useful and discarding what is destructive. They understand that criticism is inevitable and that enduring requires the ability to walk through misunderstanding without losing identity. This detachment is not coldness but strength, it is the ability to keep moving even when applause is absent. Resilience in leadership also depends on adaptability and adaptability is born from toughness. A fragile mind panics when plans collapse but a tough mind adjusts. They pivot strategies, redesign models, and find new ways to execute vision. They refuse to see change as a threat but treat it as an invitation to innovate. This mindset allows them to outlast rigid competitors who cling to outdated methods until they are irrelevant. Tough leaders therefore thrive in uncertainty because they are not attached to methods but to mission and this flexibility extends their endurance beyond normal limits. Another essential element of mental toughness is pain tolerance because business is filled with disappointments, betrayals, and losses. Those who break easily cannot lead for long. Tough leaders expect pain and prepare for it. They do not waste energy complaining about its presence but invest energy in learning from it. They see pain as tuition for mastery, a necessary cost for greatness. Instead of asking why me they ask what next. They treat pain not as a signal to stop but as proof they are stretching beyond comfort zones. This relationship with pain gives them a unique edge because when others flee discomfort they remain, and by remaining they outlast. Toughness is also revealed in how leaders handle rejection because rejection is constant in entrepreneurship. Customers will reject offers, investors will reject pitches, markets will reject products, and even friends may reject dreams. A fragile leader interprets rejection as identity failure but a tough leader interprets rejection as redirection. They extract lessons, refine approaches, and try again with greater clarity. They understand that rejection is not personal, it is situational. By refusing to internalize rejection they preserve confidence and confidence and sustains momentum. This resilience in the face of rejection builds reputation because people eventually respect leaders who refuse to be silenced. Mental toughness further expresses itself in self-control because leadership brings power and without control power corrupts and corruption destroys endurance. A tough leader disciplines appetites, regulates desires, and resists shortcuts. They understand that endurance is not only about surviving hardship but about maintaining integrity under pressure. Many businesses collapse not from external attack but from internal compromise. Leaders who lacked the toughness to say no to greed, dishonesty, or pride destroyed what they built. Enduring leaders remain unshaken because they exercise restraint when others indulge recklessly. Their consistency builds trust and trust is the currency of endurance. Another mark of toughness is the ability to handle solitude. Leadership often requires walking alone before others understand and loneliness breaks the weak. Tough leaders prepare their minds for solitude. They find strength in conviction, they anchor themselves in vision, and they draw power from inner resources when outer support is lacking. They refuse to equate being alone to being wrong. Instead they see solitude as a refining fire that clarifies motives and strengthens resolve. This capacity to walk alone makes them dangerous to discouragement because they do not collapse simply because others do not see what they see. Mental toughness is not only about surviving but about thriving under pressure. It is the ability to maintain clarity in chaos, to make progress in uncertainty, to lead with conviction in crisis. It is forged through struggle not comfort. Every obstacle that does not break the leader makes them tougher and every season of difficulty becomes training for greater responsibility. Tough leaders embrace this reality and therefore grow stronger with each storm. Ultimately mental toughness is the crown of endurance because it is what transforms persistence and resilience into lasting leadership. It is what ensures that the entrepreneur not only survives the business battlefield but builds something that endures long after the immediate battle is forgotten. Without toughness endurance fades but with toughness endurance becomes inevitable because no matter the intensity of opposition the mind that refuses to break guarantees the continuation of the journey.

5

The Unseen Cost of Quitting

In the journey of business there are many voices that encourage stopping at the first sign of discomfort and many examples of individuals who once started with passion but never endured to see results yet the unseen cost of quitting is rarely discussed in detail. People often evaluate quitting based on immediate relief such as removing themselves from stress or financial strain but what remains invisible at the moment of decision are the long term consequences that silently shape identity opportunity and legacy. When an entrepreneur quits too early they not only forfeit the current venture but also weaken their resilience muscle which is built only through sustained pressure. Just like physical strength cannot be developed without repeated resistance the strength of perseverance cannot be cultivated without facing extended trials. Every time quitting becomes the default option it programs the mind to adopt quitting as a pattern and over time this makes future endurance more difficult. The unseen cost is that people who quit too often stop believing in their own ability to complete difficult tasks. Self-doubt begins to overshadow ambition and even when a new idea emerges the voice of past quitting speaks louder than the voice of new possibilities. Another cost of quitting lies in the relationships lost along the way because investors employees and customers are not only watching what a business delivers but also observing the character of the entrepreneur. When someone abandons their vision prematurely it signals instability to those who trusted them and once trust is broken it takes a monumental effort to rebuild. Endurance communicates reliability and people gravitate toward reliable leaders. Quitting communication inconsistency and in business inconsistency is expensive. The entrepreneur who quits also forfeits the compounding effect of time which is one of the most powerful forces in enterprise growth. Many businesses that today are celebrated as industry giants were once on the verge of collapse but their founders refused to quit and in doing so they allowed time to work for them. The unseen cost of quitting is that the entrepreneur never reaches the compounding stage and instead remains trapped in a cycle of starting over. Starting over may feel exciting at first but the hidden damage is that momentum is constantly lost. Momentum is built when effort is sustained in a single direction long enough for systems to stabilize for customers to become loyal and for reputation to be established. Quitting too soon interrupts this process and makes every new beginning more fragile than the last. There is also a psychological tax that quitting imposes. Each abandoned dream leaves behind a residue of regret and regret grows heavier with time because people look back and wonder what might have been had they endured a little longer. Regret is a quiet weight that shapes choices in the future often preventing individuals from taking bold risks because they fear repeating the pattern of failure. Thus quitting today can suffocate tomorrow's opportunities. In contrast endurance transforms even failure into lessons that become assets for the future. The unseen cost of quitting is therefore not only financial or relational but existential. It touches the very question of how people see themselves and whether they truly believe they can overcome challenges. Those who quit too often shrink in their imagination because they unconsciously learn that obstacles are stronger than their will. Those who endure expand in imagination because they see proof that persistence can bend circumstances. The unseen cost of quitting is therefore the loss of proof that one is capable of surviving difficulty. Without this proof it becomes harder to inspire others because leadership in business is less about speeches and more about embodied resilience. Employees follow leaders who model commitment through storms not leaders who vanish when conditions become rough. The unseen cost of quitting also extends to society at large because every abandoned venture represents jobs that could have been created products that could have been invented or services that could have improved communities. Quitting prematurely robs not only the entrepreneur but the ecosystem of potential value. Endurance on the other hand multiplies value beyond the entrepreneur. By recognizing the hidden damage caused by quitting entrepreneurs can reframe their struggles as investments not merely for their own benefit but for the countless people connected to their vision. Understanding these unseen costs is what keeps many from giving up when logic tells them to. They realize that while endurance is painful quitting is more expensive in the long run. When others walk away those who stay are not only fighting for profits but also for self-mastery trust reputation legacy and the ripple effects of their enterprise in the world.

Building a Mindset that Outlasts the Storm

Endurance in business is not a matter of luck or circumstance but a matter of mindset and it is the shaping of this mindset that distinguishes those who thrive when others quit. A mindset that outlasts storms is not developed in one moment but forged through repeated choices that rewire the way the entrepreneur interprets pressure. At the heart of this mindset is the belief that storms are temporary but the lessons gained through perseverance are permanent. To build such a mindset the entrepreneur must first accept that challenges are not intruders but expected elements of the journey. When storms arrive instead of interpreting them as signs to withdraw the resilient mindset views them as tests that validate the seriousness of their vision. This shift is crucial because perception determines endurance. If difficulty is seen as punishment then quitting feels justified but if difficulty is seen as proof of process then perseverance becomes non-negotiable. Building a mindset that outlasts the storm requires the constant practice of reframing. For instance when sales decline the average entrepreneur sees danger but the enduring entrepreneur sees a signal to innovate marketing strategy or improve customer engagement. When competition intensifies the average entrepreneur feels threatened but the enduring entrepreneur sees validation that the market is worth pursuing and doubles efforts to differentiate. Reframing builds mental stamina because it converts fear into fuel. Another discipline that sustains a resilient mindset is self-talk. The dialogue an entrepreneur has with themselves in moments of crisis is often more powerful than external advice. If the inner voice is filled with defeat then external encouragement cannot penetrate but if the inner voice has been trained to speak faith persistence and courage then even in solitude the entrepreneur can keep moving. This is why great leaders cultivate affirmations that strengthen their endurance. They remind themselves not of what is collapsing but of what they have already survived. Each reminder of past survival becomes ammunition for future battles. In addition to reframing and self-talking the resilient mindset thrives on adaptability. A rigid mind breaks under pressure but a flexible mind bends and recovers. Entrepreneurs who endure do not expect their initial plan to unfold perfectly they anticipate revisions pivots and redefinitions as part of the process. Adaptability reduces the shock of storms because it normalizes change. When change is normalized it becomes less threatening and more manageable. This is why some entrepreneurs thrive even when their industry is disrupted because their mindset has been trained to expect disruption and harness it. Furthermore a mindset that outlasts storms is anchored in a compelling why. Those who quit often do so because their reasons for starting were shallow but those who endure draw from deep reservoirs of purpose. Purpose provides fuel when emotions run dry. When setbacks hit and motivation feels absent it is the clarity of purpose that keeps the entrepreneur moving. Purpose is the anchor that steadies the ship when waves are violent. Without a strong why even small storms can dismantle determination. With a strong even hurricanes cannot stop momentum. Building such a mindset also involves managing focus. A scattered mind is vulnerable to discouragement because it chases too many distractions but a focused mind preserves energy for the essentials. Entrepreneurs who outlast storms have learned to filter noise and prioritize what directly advances their mission. Focus protects endurance by preventing the waste of energy on irrelevant pursuits. Equally important is the cultivation of resilience rituals. These are consistent practices that fortify the mind such as journaling victories reflecting on gratitude maintaining physical health or meditating on long term goals. Resilience rituals provide stability when everything else feels unstable. They remind the entrepreneur of continuity amid chaos. Over time these rituals create an inner fortress that storms cannot penetrate easily. Community also plays a critical role in mindset building. Endurance is strengthened when surrounded by peers' mentors or teams who embody the same spirit. Isolation magnifies fear while connection multiplies courage. A resilient mindset is therefore not only personal but communal because the voices around an entrepreneur reinforce or weaken their resolve. To outlast storms entrepreneurs must be intentional about their environment because environment shapes endurance as much as effort. Ultimately building a mindset that outlasts storms is not about eliminating fear but mastering it. It is about acknowledging that fear will always appear yet choosing to act courageously in its presence. Courage is not the absence of storms but the refusal to let storms dictate direction. Those who nurture this mindset gradually transform into leaders who do not merely survive storms but harness them to grow stronger. Every storm that is outlasted becomes proof that the entrepreneur is capable of handling greater responsibilities. This proof compounds over time and eventually forms the identity of someone who cannot be easily shaken. It is this unshakable identity that becomes the ultimate asset in business because industries change competitors and rise and fall and markets evolve but the entrepreneur who has cultivated a mindset that outlasts storms remains relevant and resilient across seasons.

Converting Endurance into Advantage

Endurance in business is not only about survival it is about converting perseverance into a competitive advantage that others cannot replicate. While many entrepreneurs quit under pressure those who remain discover that endurance itself creates unique opportunities unavailable to the faint hearted. Converting endurance into advantage begins with the realization that longevity builds authority. In industries where trends change quickly consistency becomes a rare and powerful differentiator. Customers trust brands that have proven stability over time. Investors are more confident in entrepreneurs who have weathered storms and remained consistent. Endurance thus becomes a marketing tool because longevity signals credibility. The entrepreneur who endures long enough automatically separates themselves from competitors who disappeared. This separation is an advantage because reputation compounds with every year of consistent operation. Beyond credibility endurance breeds expertise. Challenges that once felt overwhelming eventually become familiar territory for the enduring entrepreneur. Each obstacle teaches new strategies each failure sharpens decision making each survival strengthens intuition. Over time the enduring entrepreneur accumulates wisdom that competitors who quit will never gain. This wisdom becomes a strategic advantage because it allows the entrepreneur to anticipate problems others cannot see and to navigate complexity with calm confidence. Endurance also unlocks opportunities that are invisible in the short term. Many partnerships contracts and networks are only open to those who have demonstrated staying power. Stakeholders prefer aligning with entrepreneurs who have a proven history of resilience because they know these individuals will not abandon commitments halfway. By enduring an entrepreneur enters circles of trust that are close to those who treat business as a seasonal experiment. Another way endurance becomes an advantage is through resource efficiency. The longer one endures the more refined their systems become. Processes that once consumed excessive energy are optimized mistakes that once drained finances are avoided and networks that once had to be built from scratch now provide steady support. The entrepreneur who endures long enough begins to operate with less waste and greater effectiveness. This efficiency translates into stronger margins and greater scalability. Endurance also allows entrepreneurs to witness cycles that newcomers cannot predict. Markets often move in patterns and only those who remain long enough can identify these cycles and position themselves to benefit. For example an entrepreneur who has endured through multiple recessions develops strategies to thrive during downturns while competitors' panic. This cyclical insight is a hidden advantage that cannot be learned in theory but only through lived endurance. Furthermore endurance reshapes brand identity. A brand that has survived storms automatically communicates resilience and customers resonate with resilience because it mirrors their own struggles. People admire and remain loyal to brands that reflect their values. Endurance gives a brand narrative depth. Instead of being another product or service it becomes a symbol of determination. This symbolic power converts endurance into emotional equity and emotional equity is one of the most valuable forms of capital in business. Converting endurance into advantage also means leveraging the trust it builds. Trust once established creates exponential opportunities. Loyal customers become advocates attracting new clients at no extra cost. Satisfied partners provide referrals. Investors reinvest confidently. Trust opens doors that money cannot always buy. This trust is not built in a day but earned through consistent endurance. Additionally the entrepreneur who endures long enough begins to shape industry standards. Competitors start looking to them for cues markets adjust to their presence and their persistence creates a gravitational pull that influences trends. This kind of influence is the ultimate advantage because it positions the entrepreneur not just as a participant in the market but as a shaper of it. Endurance thus becomes power. Yet converting endurance into advantage requires intentional reflection. Endurance alone without strategy can lead to stagnation. It is not enough to simply last one must learn actively from every season endured and convert these lessons into innovations. The most successful entrepreneurs are those who endure and evolve simultaneously. They do not just stay in the game they rise to new levels through the credibility expertise efficiency trust and influence that endurance provides. The advantage is not only personal but generational because businesses built on endurance outlive their founders. They transition into legacies that impact future leaders. Converting endurance into advantage is therefore the highest expression of thriving when others quit because it means survival has been transformed into strength and persistence has been translated into power.

6

The Burden and Blessing of Patience

Patience is one of the most underrated virtues in business yet it remains the invisible thread that holds endurance together and separates those who thrive from those who collapse. Many entrepreneurs mistakenly equate patience with passivity but patience is not about waiting idly it is about holding steady while actively pursuing a vision through changing seasons. The burden of patience is heavy because in a world where instant gratification dominates and results are expected at lightning speed the entrepreneur must resist the temptation to measure progress by daily fluctuations. It is easy to celebrate quick wins but patience demands celebrating consistency instead of speed. To carry the burden of patience means enduring long periods when results do not align with effort and choosing to believe that hidden growth is still occurring. Patience is tested most severely when setbacks create doubt and when peers appear to be advancing faster. The burden intensifies when financial constraints make it difficult to sustain operations or when recognition is delayed for years.

It is a burden because it demands suppressing the natural human desire for immediate validation. Yet within this burden lies the blessing because patience builds resilience and resilience is a currency no competitor can counterfeit. Those who have cultivated patience develop an inner calm that allows them to make decisions from clarity rather than panic. This calmness becomes a strategic advantage when markets shift or when crises erupt. While impatient entrepreneurs rush into impulsive decisions that create deeper problems those who embrace patience observe carefully adjust strategically and act with foresight. The blessing of patience also lies in its ability to protect against premature quitting. Many businesses collapse not because the idea was flawed but because the founder lacked the patience to let it mature. Seeds do not sprout overnight and ideas need incubation time. The entrepreneur who endures through the silent seasons discovers that breakthroughs are often delayed rewards for unseen persistence. The blessing is that when growth finally manifests it does so with a compounding effect that exceeds initial expectations. Patience also sharpens perception because waiting teaches attentiveness. An impatient person overlooks subtle shifts in customer behavior or emerging opportunities but a patient entrepreneur sees it beneath the surface. They recognize trends before they become mainstream because they have been observing with depth rather than rushing from one distraction to another. This perception transforms patience into wisdom and wisdom into strategy. Yet patience must not be confused with stagnation. Enduring entrepreneurs practice active patience which means they keep building systems nurturing relationships refining products and expanding knowledge even while waiting for visible success. This form of patience transforms waiting into preparation and when opportunity finally arrives the entrepreneur is ready to maximize it. The blessing of patience also extends to the personal growth of the entrepreneur. Waiting stretches character teaches humility perseverance empathy and self-control. These virtues enrich leadership because they build credibility among teams and partners. People trust leaders who do not crumble under delay. They admire those who remain steady and consistent even when results are not immediate. Therefore patience is not only a burden to be endured but a blessing that enriches every dimension of the entrepreneurial journey. Those who master patience discover that while others quit in frustration they themselves are quietly building the roots of a legacy that time will eventually reveal.

Resilience as a Renewable Resource

Resilience is often spoken of as if it were a fixed trait something a person either has or lacks but in reality resilience is a renewable resource that grows with use. The enduring entrepreneur understands that resilience is not depleted permanently by hardship but rather replenished through intentional recovery and perspective. To thrive when others quit requires a deep understanding of how to continuously renew resilience because business is not a single challenge but an unending series of challenges. Every season brings new storms and without renewal even the strongest entrepreneur eventually burns out. The renewable nature of resilience begins with self-awareness. An entrepreneur must recognize the early signs of depletion such as cynicism lack of creativity or emotional fatigue. Instead of interpreting these signs as proof of weakness the enduring entrepreneur sees them as signals to replenish. Renewal often comes from rest yet rest must be intentional because many entrepreneurs mistakenly believe that working harder without pause is the only path to progress. In truth overextension erodes resilience while strategic rest multiplies it. Sleep exercise reflection and time in nourishing environments restore the mind and body making resilience ready for the next challenge. Another dimension of renewal lies in reframing adversity. Resilience is depleted when challenges are viewed as personal attacks but it is renewed when challenges are interpreted as training. By seeing every difficulty as an opportunity to grow skills or refine strategies the entrepreneur transforms stress into fuel. This mental alchemy keeps resilience renewable because it prevents despair from taking root. Community is another powerful source of renewal. Endurance is not sustained in isolation but multiplied in connection. Mentor's peers and supportive networks remind the entrepreneur that they are not alone in the struggle and shared stories of perseverance and reignite resilience. The voices of those who have survived similar storms provide reassurance that renewal is possible. In addition resilience is renewed by purpose. When entrepreneurs reconnect with the core reason they began their journey they rediscover energy that seemed lost. Purpose functions like a reservoir that can be tapped in moments of exhaustion. It refuels determination because it reminds the entrepreneur that their effort matters beyond immediate discomfort. Creativity is also a form of renewal because it reintroduces joy into the grind. Engaging in innovative thinking experimenting with new solutions or revisiting forgotten passions replenishes enthusiasm and strengthens resilience. Renewal requires balance between persistence and flexibility. Resilience is drained when entrepreneurs stubbornly hold on to failing methods but it is renewed when they adapt without abandoning the larger vision. Adaptability keeps resilience fresh because it prevents stagnation. Furthermore resilience renewal often requires celebrating small victories. Many entrepreneurs focus so much on future goals that they ignore progress already made. By acknowledging milestones however minor they create positive reinforcement that rejuvenates spirit. Resilience thrives on gratitude because gratitude amplifies perspective reminding the entrepreneur of how far they have already come. The renewable nature of resilience proves that no entrepreneur is doomed to permanent depletion. Those who learn to replenish continually can endure indefinitely. They become unbreakable not because they never get tired but because they know how to recover. This makes resilience not only a shield against failure but also a renewable engine for growth. Entrepreneurs who harness resilience as a renewable resource discover that every storm that survived does not leave them weaker but stronger and more prepared for the next.

The Legacy of Endurance

Endurance in business is never only about the present moment it is about the legacy that endures beyond the entrepreneur's lifetime. The legacy of endurance is built when choices made today create ripples that continue to influence generations long after the original struggle has been forgotten. To understand the legacy of endurance one must first recognize that every decision to persist shapes culture within and beyond the business. Employees observing a leader who refuses to quit learn that resilience is not optional but expected. This culture outlives the immediate challenge because it conditions people to respond to future trials with the same spirit of perseverance. Over time a company built on endurance becomes a beacon in its industry attracting individuals who value stability and trust. The legacy therefore begins as an internal culture but expands into external influence. Customers also experience the legacy of endurance because consistency builds trust. A business that remains reliable through decades of change communicates to its customers that it is not a fleeting experiment but a committed partner in their journey. This reliability creates loyalty that extends through families and communities. Entire generations can grow up trusting a brand because its founders chose endurance over quitting. Beyond reputation the legacy of endurance also manifests in the innovations that persistence unlocks. Many groundbreaking discoveries and transformative products were born not from instant genius but from years of sustained effort. When entrepreneurs endure through failure after failure they eventually produce breakthroughs that reshape industries. These breakthroughs become part of the legacy because they outlast the temporary struggles that produced them. The legacy also lies in the stories told. Every enduring entrepreneur leaves behind narratives that inspire future dreamers. A young entrepreneur years from now may draw courage not from abstract theory but from the concrete story of someone who endured when it was easier to quit. These stories become inheritance for society reminding each generation that greatness is never achieved without endurance. The legacy of endurance is also financial. Businesses that survive storms create wealth not only for their founders but for employees' shareholders and communities. This wealth funds education healthcare innovation and opportunity. The ripple effects transform societies because one person's choice to endure created economic ecosystems that sustain others. Yet the most profound aspect of the legacy of endurance is personal transformation. The entrepreneur who endures emerges not only as a business leader but as a model of human potential. Their character integrity and resilience become part of their identity and these qualities continue to inspire even after their enterprise has evolved or ended. Their legacy is written not only in profits but in lives touched. Endurance ensures that the sacrifices made were not in vain because the fruits continue to multiply beyond the immediate season. Those who quit rarely leave legacies worth remembering because they surrendered their potential before it matured. But those who endure give future generations proof that persistence is more powerful than adversity. The legacy of endurance therefore is the greatest reward of thriving in business when others quit. It is the confirmation that struggles survived today will echo as strength tomorrow and that the choice to endure creates a story that time itself cannot erase.

7

The Discipline of Consistency

Consistency is the lifeblood of endurance and the silent power that transforms ordinary businesses into enduring institutions. Many entrepreneurs begin with bursts of passion and short term energy but passion without consistency is like fire without fuel it burns bright for a moment and fades into ash. The discipline of consistency demands more than excitement it requires deliberate repetition of essential actions even when enthusiasm has disappeared. Consistency is difficult because the human mind craves novelty and avoids monotony yet in business it is the repeated small actions performed daily that create compound impact. An entrepreneur who commits to consistency understands that every day of showing up builds a foundation brick by brick. One of the greatest challenges in business is that results rarely match effort in the short term and this mismatch convinces many to abandon their routines. They work diligently for a season then grow weary when returns are not immediate. Consistency resists this temptation by anchoring itself not in outcomes but in process. The consistent entrepreneur wakes up and does the necessary work whether recognition comes or not. This steady commitment builds credibility with team investors and customers because they learn to trust that the entrepreneur is dependable. Trust is the currency of business and consistency is the mint where that currency is produced. Without consistency even great ideas collapse because execution becomes unreliable. With consistency even average ideas can thrive because persistence improves them over time. The discipline of consistency also protects against the destructive power of mood swings. Everyone faces days of doubt discouragement or exhaustion. If business is driven by emotion then momentum collapses whenever motivation declines. Consistency bypasses emotion by turning key actions into non-negotiable habits. Habits stabilize effort so that progress is maintained even in low energy seasons. This is why athletes train daily regardless of weather or mood because consistency builds muscle memory that does not rely on inspiration. Entrepreneurs must train their business muscles the same way by institutionalizing routines that guarantee progress. Consistency also reveals patterns that would otherwise remain invisible. Data collected over time becomes meaningful only when actions are sustained long enough to create a body of evidence. Sporadic efforts produce noise but consistent actions produce clarity. By maintaining steady marketing campaigns consistent customer engagement and reliable product quality entrepreneurs gather feedback that informs better strategy. This iterative cycle strengthens the enterprise in ways that randomness never could. Furthermore consistency signals seriousness. Investors and partners hesitate to commit to entrepreneurs who lack follow through but when they see years of consistent effort their confidence grows. A consistent presence in the market communicates durability, which is often more persuasive than exaggerated promises. Customers too are drawn to consistency because it creates reliability. A customer who knows that a business will deliver the same quality every time remains loyal. Loyalty compounds into advocacy and advocacy into growth. Consistency also sharpens skill. Mastery in any field is achieved not through occasional effort but through relentless practice. Each day of consistent effort builds competence that cannot be replicated by shortcuts. This competence becomes an unspoken advantage because while competitors quit or fluctuate the consistent entrepreneur keeps improving steadily. Eventually the gap in skill and reputation becomes unbridgeable. Yet consistency is not automatic it is a discipline that must be chosen repeatedly. Distractions tempt entrepreneurs to chase every new trend but discipline says stay the course until results manifest. Discipline also demands accountability because consistency is fragile in isolation. Entrepreneurs who hold themselves accountable to mentor's peers or systems sustain routines longer than those who rely on willpower alone. Accountability creates external reinforcement for internal commitment. Ultimately consistency transforms endurance from a vague aspiration into a tangible habit. It ensures that when others quit the entrepreneur still shows up. Over time this discipline compounds into a reputation of reliability and mastery. The discipline of consistency is therefore the quiet engine of thriving in business and the invisible armor that protects against premature collapse.

The Energy of Adaptability

Endurance does not mean stubbornly clinging to one method it means sustaining commitment to a vision while adapting methods as circumstances evolve. The energy of adaptability distinguishes survivors from those who vanish at the first sign of disruption. In a business world where markets shift technologies evolve and customer preferences change adaptability is not optional it is essential. Yet adaptability is not simply reactionary it is proactive flexibility guided by clarity of purpose. The energy of adaptability flows from the willingness to see change not as threat but as opportunity. Entrepreneurs who resist change often drain their own strength because they waste energy fighting inevitable realities. Those who embrace adaptability conserve energy by flowing with change and redirecting momentum toward innovation. Adaptability begins with humility because it requires admitting that initial strategies may no longer be sufficient. Many entrepreneurs collapse because pride convinces them that altering their approach is weakness. In truth adaptability is strength because it demonstrates awareness and agility. Adapting does not mean abandoning vision it means adjusting the route without losing sight of the destination. The enduring entrepreneur treats business like navigation through unpredictable weather. When winds shift a rigid sailor is stranded but an adaptable sailor adjusts sails and continues forward. Similarly adaptability allows the entrepreneur to maintain direction despite turbulence. The energy of adaptability also comes from curiosity. Those who remain curious continually study trends technologies and customer behaviors. This curiosity equips them to anticipate change rather than react to it. They stay ahead of competitors because they are not blindsided by shifts but prepared to harness them. Adaptability transforms uncertainty into an advantage because it positions entrepreneurs as innovators who can thrive in any climate. Another source of adaptability energy is experimentation. Enduring entrepreneurs do not fear trial and error they embrace it as part of discovery. They test new models to explore fresh partnerships and refine products through iteration. Each experiment may not succeed but it provides data that strengthens the next attempt. Adaptability therefore thrives on learning and every failure becomes a lesson fueling progress. Adaptability also demands emotional resilience because change often provokes fear. Fear convinces many to retreat but adaptable entrepreneurs regulate fear by focusing on possibilities instead of losses. They train themselves to see what could be gained through change rather than what might be lost. This mindset sustains enthusiasm and turns adaptability into energy rather than exhaustion. Furthermore adaptability enhances customer connection because customers trust businesses that evolve with their needs. A company that adapts demonstrates that it listens and responds. This responsiveness builds loyalty and makes customers partners in innovation. The energy of adaptability thus multiplies because it is reinforced by external validation from those being served. In addition adaptability builds strategic partnerships because flexible businesses are easier to collaborate with. Partners prefer entrepreneurs who can adjust to new realities instead of rigidly insisting on outdated models. Such flexibility fosters long term alliances that expand influence and market presence. Adaptability also safeguards against irrelevance. Many once dominant companies collapsed because they refused to adapt to technological or cultural shifts. Entrepreneurs who embody adaptability not only survive these shifts but often lead them. Their willingness to change becomes a competitive edge because it positions them as thought leaders rather than laggards. The energy of adaptability also protects mental health. Rigid entrepreneurs constantly feel attacked by change while adaptable ones see change as natural. This reduces stress and sustains momentum. By flowing with evolution instead of resisting it they conserve emotional energy for creation. Ultimately the energy of adaptability fuels endurance by ensuring that persistence is not stagnant but dynamic. It ensures that thriving in business is not about clinging to old ways but about reinventing methods without abandoning mission. Entrepreneurs who master adaptability become unshakable because no disruption can eliminate their relevance. Their energy renews with each adaptation making them not only survivors but leaders in ever changing landscapes.

The Courage to Be Different

At the core of endurance lies the courage to be different because thriving when others quit often means standing apart from common expectations and resisting the gravitational pull of conformity. The courage to be different is not about rebellion for its own sake it is about remaining true to a vision even when the majority dismisses it. In business difference often provokes resistance because society rewards predictability while innovation requires deviation. Entrepreneurs who thrive understand that enduring difference is uncomfortable yet necessary. Courage is required because being different invites criticism skepticism and isolation. Friends may not understand family may doubt and peers may mock yet the enduring entrepreneur draws strength not from acceptance but from conviction. The courage to be different is therefore both shield and compass shielding against external doubt while guiding decisions when the path ahead is uncharted. Difference is powerful because it creates distinction in crowded markets. Customers are drawn to businesses that dare to stand out by offering unique value rather than copying trends. This uniqueness is not born of luck but of courageous commitment to authenticity. The entrepreneur who endures understands that imitation may provide temporary acceptance but only originality creates lasting relevance. To embody difference requires resilience because the early stages of innovation are often met with rejection. History is filled with entrepreneurs whose ideas were dismissed as impossible until persistence proved otherwise. The courage to be different fuels endurance through these seasons of ridicule because it reminds the entrepreneur that true value is rarely recognized immediately. Courage also transforms fear into creativity. When others fear stepping outside conventions the courageous entrepreneur experiments boldly and these experiments often lead to breakthroughs. By daring to be different the entrepreneur creates new markets or redefines old ones. This courage is contagious, inspiring teams to think boldly and customers to trust the vision. The courage to be different is also ethical because it prevents compromise of core values for temporary gain. Many entrepreneurs quit or collapse because they bend principles to match trends but those who endure have the courage to stand firm even when it costs them short term profit. This integrity builds a brand that customers respect and trust long term. Courage also protects against mediocrity because mediocrity thrives on sameness while excellence demands distinction. Enduring entrepreneurs accept the discomfort of being misunderstood because they know that clarity eventually emerges. Over time their courage becomes a narrative of inspiration proving that difference is not weakness but strength. The courage to be different also enables long term positioning. While competitors chase short term fads the courageous entrepreneur invests in vision that may take years to mature. This foresight is only possible because courage silences fear of delay. Enduring entrepreneurs understand that true impact is not measured by immediate applause but by lasting influence. Courage allows them to endure the silence until the echo of their difference reshapes industries. Furthermore the courage to be different creates legacies because legacies are never built by those who blend in but by those who dared to stand apart. The entrepreneurs remembered across history are those who endured ridicule in their time to give the world something it did not yet understand. Courage is therefore the seed of legacy because it ensures that endurance has purpose. To thrive in business when others quit requires this rare courage because without it endurance degenerates into survival but with it endurance becomes transformation. The courage to be different is thus the highest expression of entrepreneurial perseverance because it affirms that thriving is not only about lasting longer than others but about leaving a mark that could not have been made by conformity.

8

The Weight of Responsibility

Endurance in business is inseparable from responsibility because the longer an enterprise survives the more weight rests on the shoulders of its founder and leaders. Responsibility is the unspoken cost of growth because with every new client every new employee and all new investor the entrepreneur's choices expand in consequence. Many who begin the journey of business underestimate this reality. They imagine entrepreneurship as freedom from control but in truth endurance binds the entrepreneur to accountability. Responsibility is heavy because it demands sacrifice and consistency not only for self but for others whose livelihoods and futures depend on the health of the enterprise. This weight is why endurance requires a strong spine because responsibility tests resolve more than ambition ever does. Carrying responsibility means that an entrepreneur cannot afford reckless decisions. Every strategic move must be weighed not just against personal interest but against collective wellbeing. Employees look to the entrepreneur for stability. Families of employees rely on the company for sustenance. Investors trust that capital will be preserved and multiplied. Customers expect quality and reliability. Responsibility therefore is not an abstract virtue it is a daily demand pressing against the entrepreneur's endurance. This weight can feel crushing when setbacks arise because failure in business does not simply affect the entrepreneur alone it ripples outward into many lives. Some entrepreneurs collapse under this pressure because they view responsibility as a burden. Those who endure shift perspective and see it as privilege. They realize that responsibility is proof of trust and trust is earned only by consistency and integrity. This mental shift transforms responsibility from oppression into fuel. The weight becomes the anchor that steadies commitment when storms come. It prevents abandonment because the entrepreneur knows too many depend on their persistence. Responsibility also sharpens decision making because weight compels wisdom. Without responsibility choices can be impulsive but with responsibility choices must be deliberate. Enduring entrepreneurs develop the ability to delay gratification not because it pleases them but because it sustains others. They embrace discipline over desire. They sacrifice leisure for diligence. They accept scrutiny as a price for stewardship. This maturity becomes part of the enterprise's identity and creates a culture of accountability that outlasts the founder. The weight of responsibility is also emotional. Leaders who endure often feel the invisible pressure of expectations. They cannot express doubt openly lest it weaken team morale yet they too face moments of uncertainty. Endurance requires learning how to manage personal fear without projecting instability. It means finding strength in private battles while exuding confidence in public ones. This dual weight can exhaust but it also refines character. Responsibility teaches patience, humility and empathy because it forces leaders to think beyond themselves. The longer responsibility is carried the stronger endurance grows because the leader becomes accustomed to standing firm under load. Just as muscles grow by lifting heavier weights endurance grows by bearing larger responsibilities. Responsibility also clarifies purpose. Entrepreneurs who focus solely on profit often lose motivation when profits shrink but those who embrace responsibility find drive in service. They continue not because circumstances are favorable but because they understand abandonment would betray those who trust them. This sense of duty becomes the compass of endurance and transforms survival into stewardship. Furthermore responsibility protects against arrogance. Success can intoxicate but responsibility sobers. Knowing that decisions carry consequences tempers pride and sustains humility. Humility itself fuels endurance because it keeps the entrepreneur teachable and adaptable. In this way responsibility is paradoxical. Though it feels heavy it actually lightens the entrepreneur's path by anchoring them in values and forcing maturity. The weight of responsibility is therefore not an obstacle to endurance but its very proof because only those willing to carry it can thrive when others quit.

The Power of Sacrifice

Endurance is impossible without sacrifice because thriving beyond ordinary limits requires surrendering comforts conveniences and at times even immediate desires. Sacrifice is the currency of growth. Every enterprise that stands tall is built upon layers of invisible sacrifices made by those who refused to quit. The power of sacrifice lies in its ability to exchange something small for something greater. In the beginning sacrifice often looks unreasonable to outsiders. Friends cannot understand why the entrepreneur refuses social pleasures to work long nights. Family cannot understand why secure employment is abandoned for uncertain ventures. Critics cannot understand why the entrepreneur pours resources into ideas that may fail. Yet sacrifice is the silent language of belief. It says I am willing to pay today for what tomorrow requires. Those unwilling to sacrifice rarely endure because business will always demand payment upfront before yielding reward. Sacrifice is painful because it involves loss but endurance transforms loss into investment. Time lost in leisure is time invested in learning. Money lost in experimentation is money invested in innovation. Comfort lost in sleepless nights is comfort invested in resilience. Sacrifice is the seed and endurance is the soil in which it grows until harvest comes. Enduring entrepreneurs know that sacrifice is not occasional but continual. The power of sacrifice is that it reshapes identity. Each act of giving up build's toughness. The entrepreneur becomes the kind of person who can survive what others cannot. They train their mind and body to accept discomfort as normal. This adaptation makes them formidable because challenges that break others simply meet someone already accustomed to hard cost. Sacrifice also purifies intention. Many begin business for quick gain but sacrifice filters motives. When months of labor yield little and yet the entrepreneur persists by giving more it reveals whether they truly believe in vision. This authenticity attracts allies because people trust those who bleed for their cause. Teams follow leaders who prove through sacrifice that they are invested beyond convenience. Investors respect founders who have personally sacrificed resources because they show commitment. Customers resonate with brands that have endured visible hardship to deliver value. Thus sacrifice multiplies influence because it validates sincerity. Sacrifice also produces perspective. It teaches that nothing worth keeping comes cheap. By sacrificing the entrepreneur learns patience because rewards take time. They learn gratitude because each gain represents cost. They learn empathy because they understand struggle. This perspective prevents entitlement and cultivates appreciation for every stage of growth. Furthermore sacrifice builds resilience. Each sacrifice is like fire that hardens steel. Entrepreneurs who have given much are not easily shaken because they know they have survived costly seasons. They view challenges not as final but as familiar. They remind themselves that if past sacrifices were endured then present trials can also be survived. Sacrifice therefore becomes memory fuel for endurance. The power of sacrifice is also contagious. Teams emulate leaders who sacrifice. When employees see leaders willing to work late, forgo luxury and carry burdens they too commit deeper. Culture is shaped not by slogans but by sacrifices visible to all. A culture of sacrifice sustains enterprises because it creates shared ownership of hardship and triumph. Sacrifice also sets apart. Competitors may mimic strategy but few will match sacrifice. This becomes a barrier of endurance because sacrifice weeds out pretenders. Those unwilling to sacrifice cannot outlast those who make it a lifestyle. Over time sacrifice produces compounding returns. What was surrendered years ago blossoms into strength influence and legacy. Sacrifice may feel like loss in the moment but endurance transforms it into power. Ultimately the power of sacrifice lies in its ability to anchor entrepreneurs when rewards delay because sacrifice itself becomes the reward. To know that one gave everything and still stood is the greatest fuel for persistence. The power of sacrifice is the unshakable foundation of thriving in business when others quit.

The Reward of Legacy

Endurance without legacy is survival but endurance with legacy is victory. The true reward of thriving when others quit is not merely profit but the legacy that endures after the entrepreneur is gone. Legacy is the imprint left on people industries and communities because of persistence. It is the unseen reward that outlives wealth and fame. Legacy matters because businesses that endure transform into institutions that continue shaping lives long after the founder's presence. The reward of legacy gives endurance meaning because it shifts focus from temporary gains to eternal impact. Entrepreneurs who endure with legacy in mind live for something greater than themselves. They ask not only how I can succeed but how can my success serve others even when I am absent. This perspective fuels endurance because it provides purpose during weary seasons. Legacy becomes the North Star guiding decisions when fatigue tempts abandonment. The reward of legacy is that it multiplies influence. While profit benefits those directly involved legacy benefits generations. An entrepreneur who builds responsibly ensures that future employees find work, future leaders find inspiration and future customers find value. This compounding effect is the reward that makes sacrifice worthwhile. Legacy is not built by chance but by intentional choices rooted in endurance. It requires building systems that can function beyond the founder. It requires training successors who can carry vision forward. It requires embedding values into culture so that the company's identity survives transitions. Entrepreneurs who endure long enough to think legacy act differently. They prioritize sustainability over shortcuts. They choose ethics over expedience. They invest in people rather than exploiting them. These choices may slow immediate gains but they secure long term survival. Legacy is also the reward of consistency. Customers remember businesses that remain faithful to their promise over decades. Communities remember companies that invest in their wellbeing over time. Employees remember leaders who cared beyond profit. Such memories become reputation and reputation becomes heritage. The reward of legacy is therefore intangible yet priceless. Legacy also transforms personal endurance into collective endurance. When teams understand they are part of something that will outlive them they commit deeper. They work not only for wages but for meaning. This shared vision creates resilience because people fight harder for causes they believe will endure. Thus legacy multiplies strength because it enlarges purpose. Furthermore legacy turns pain into story. Sacrifices made along the way become testimonies that inspire others. Failures endured become lessons that guide successors. Every struggle becomes part of a narrative that proves endurance is worthwhile. Stories shape culture and culture preserves memory. This is why legacies outlast individuals because the stories of their endurance become part of collective identity. Legacy also redefines success. Instead of being measured by wealth alone it is measured by the difference made. Wealth fades influence remains. Entrepreneurs who endure long enough to leave legacy understand that true success is not what they took from the world but what they left behind. Legacy is reward because it ensures that the entrepreneur's endurance was not wasted on fleeting applause but invested in timeless contribution. Ultimately the reward of legacy is that it turns business into history. It transforms ordinary effort into extraordinary memory. To endure when others quit is commendable but to endure and leave legacy is incomparable. It means that the entrepreneur's life was not just about surviving seasons but about creating something that will continue serving long after the seasons end. This is the ultimate reward of endurance because while others are forgotten those who leave legacy remain forever written in the story of enterprise.

9

Building Unshakable Confidence

E ndurance in business depends greatly on the presence of unshakable confidence because confidence is the internal voice that speaks possibility when circumstances scream defeat. Without confidence the entrepreneur quits too soon because doubt amplifies every obstacle and magnifies every mistake. Yet with confidence endurance becomes natural because the leader believes in the legitimacy of their vision and the sufficiency of their capacity to navigate storms. Confidence is not arrogance and it is not ignorance. It is not blind optimism detached from reality but a disciplined conviction built from preparation, resilience, and clarity of purpose. Confidence sustains entrepreneurs through seasons when evidence of success is scarce because it is the anchor of belief that assures them that persistence is not in vain. Unshakable confidence begins with self-awareness. Entrepreneurs who endure know who they are, what they value, and what strengths they possess. This self-knowledge immunizes them against comparison because they are not chasing someone else's path but running their own race. They are not shaken when competitors move faster or when others receive applause because they are rooted in the confidence that their unique abilities and strategies matter. This confidence liberates them from envy and distraction, enabling focus on execution rather than obsession with perception. Enduring confidence is also nurtured by competence. Preparation fuels confidence because knowledge of one's craft breeds certainty. Entrepreneurs who invest time in learning their industry, understanding their customers, and refining their skills naturally project confidence because they know they are equipped. Competence transforms fear into assurance because when challenges arise they do not collapse into panic but recall the depth of preparation already accomplished. Thus confidence is not a fragile emotion but a product of diligence. The unshakable confidence that sustains endurance is built daily through discipline. Another foundation of confidence is memory. Those who endure recall victories already won. They remember challenges previously overcome and find strength in that history. This memory serves as evidence that survival is possible even when present storms rage fiercely. A tough season becomes less intimidating when the entrepreneur recalls they have walked through worse before. Confidence draws strength from such memory, converting the past into fuel for the future. This practice ensures that temporary failures do not distort perspective. Unshakable confidence is also anchored in vision. Entrepreneurs who endure are confident not because conditions are favorable but because they see beyond conditions. They hold an image of future success so vivid that temporary setbacks cannot erase it. Vision stabilizes confidence because it reminds the leader that what is seen now is not final. Confidence in vision allows them to interpret failure not as death but as detour. This ability to reframe obstacles strengthens endurance because it prevents discouragement from suffocating motivation. The confidence that endures is also relational.

It grows when entrepreneurs surround themselves with people who believe in them. Isolation weakens confidence because self-doubt multiplies in solitude but affirmation from trusted allies strengthens resolve. This does not mean depending on applause but drawing encouragement from strategic circles of truth tellers who remind the entrepreneur of capacity when discouragement attempts to deceive. This relational confidence multiplies strength because shared belief amplifies personal conviction. Confidence is also preserved by integrity. Entrepreneurs who compromise easily lose confidence because guilt and hypocrisy corrode inner assurance. Enduring entrepreneurs build confidence by aligning values with actions. When they speak they trust themselves because they live what they declare. This inner harmony becomes an unshakable base. No external critic can destabilize a leader who is at peace with their conscience. This moral confidence sustains endurance because storms may strip material possessions but cannot touch inner integrity. Unshakable confidence is not absence of fear but mastery of fear. Enduring entrepreneurs feel fear but refuse to be controlled by it. They act despite trembling because confidence interprets fear as normal resistance rather than fatal signal. By consistently acting in the presence of fear confidence grows until fear loses its grip. Thus confidence is developed not in calm waters but in turbulent seas. The more the entrepreneur survives storms the more confidence solidifies. Ultimately unshakable confidence becomes the shield of endurance. It protects against doubt, delays, and discouragement. It allows the entrepreneur to remain standing when others collapse because they are convinced deeply that persistence will yield reward.

The Discipline of Consistency

If endurance is a marathon then consistency is the rhythm that carries the entrepreneur forward when energy is low. Without consistency bursts of effort accomplish little because endurance is not about intensity in moments but about persistence over time. The discipline of consistency is what transforms ordinary actions into extraordinary results because repetition compounds into mastery and mastery translates into resilience. Entrepreneurs who endure understand that talent excites but consistency sustains. Many businesses start with flair and creative energy but collapse because enthusiasm without routine fades. The discipline of consistency ensures that even when passion wanes progress continues because systems not feelings guide action. This discipline begins with habits. Habits are the invisible architecture of endurance because they create structure where chaos could reign. Enduring entrepreneurs craft routines that align with vision. They rise early not because mornings are magical but because structure builds stability. They review goals daily not because goals are new but because repetition engrains focus. They practice diligence not occasionally but relentlessly because consistency converts small efforts into monumental achievements over time. Consistency is hard because it demands discipline against boredom. The mind craves novelty but endurance thrives on repetition. Entrepreneurs who master consistency embrace monotony as necessary. They know that greatness is often boring in practice though glamorous in result. They resist the urge to constantly change direction simply to escape routine. Instead they find creativity within discipline. This mindset transforms consistency from prison into path. The discipline of consistency also protects against burnout. Erratic bursts of activity drain energy quickly but steady consistent progress sustains strength. Like pacing in a marathon consistency ensures that the entrepreneur does not exhaust themselves too soon. This discipline distributes energy wisely, allowing recovery while maintaining forward movement. Thus endurance is safeguarded because progress never halts even in low seasons. Consistency also builds credibility. Customers trust businesses that deliver reliably. Employees respect leaders who act consistently. Investors commit to ventures that display predictable performance. Consistency therefore becomes currency because it creates expectation and expectation strengthens relationships. An entrepreneur who practices consistency may not be flashy but will always be respected because reliability is rare. The discipline of consistency also enhances resilience because repetition toughens the mind. Each repeated action builds capacity to handle more. Just as muscles strengthen with consistent exercise the entrepreneur's resolve strengthens with consistent discipline. Over time what once felt impossible becomes routine and what once demanded courage becomes automatic. This growth fuels endurance because the entrepreneur expands capacity without noticing. Consistency is also an antidote to distraction. When routine governs action external noise loses influence. The entrepreneur no longer reacts impulsively to trends but maintains direction because discipline anchors them. In a world of constant change this consistency becomes competitive advantage because while others chase novelty the enduring entrepreneur steadily builds legacy. Furthermore consistency magnifies impact because it multiplies output. A little effort daily produces more than intense effort sporadically. Endurance is therefore built not through dramatic bursts but through sustained constancy. Entrepreneurs who embrace this truth understand that small daily steps eventually cover vast distances. They are patient enough to trust the process because they know consistency guarantees arrival. The discipline of consistency is not glamorous but it is powerful. It is what separates those who last from those who fade because while others rely on fleeting motivation enduring entrepreneurs rely on systems that carry them through valleys and mountains alike. Ultimately the discipline of consistency is the secret rhythm of endurance because it ensures that the journey continues regardless of mood circumstance or opposition.

Thriving Beyond Survival

Endurance is not merely surviving storms but thriving through them. Many businesses endure yet remain stagnant because they focus only on survival. True endurance is revealed in thriving beyond survival by turning adversity into opportunity and difficulty into innovation. Thriving means using challenges as platforms for growth rather than treating them as obstacles to escape. It requires a mindset that interprets every crisis as a chance to advance. Entrepreneurs who thrive beyond survival do not ask how I can escape this storm but how can I harness this storm to sail further. This orientation transforms endurance from passive waiting into active thriving. Thriving beyond survival demands creativity because endurance without growth is merely delayed collapse. Creativity ensures that the entrepreneur evolves. In markets that constantly shift endurance without innovation guarantees irrelevance. Thriving entrepreneurs use constraints as sparks for invention. They see scarcity as a teacher that forces efficiency. They see failure as a map that reveals new direction. This creativity allows them not only to survive crises but to emerge stronger because each storm refines their capacity. Thriving also requires vision that transcends the present. Those who focus only on immediate survival make desperate choices that compromise the future. Those who thrive look beyond urgency and align strategies with long term sustainability. They invest in research, relationships, and resilience even when resources feel scarce because they know survival is insufficient. Thriving demands multiplication. While survival preserves what exists thriving expands what is possible. It is the capacity to grow in hostile environments and to prosper under pressure. This separates enduring entrepreneurs from merely surviving entrepreneurs. Thriving beyond survival also rests on optimism. Not shallow optimism that denies difficulty but resilient optimism that sees potential within difficulty. This optimism fuels morale for both leaders and team. It infuses energy when exhaustion looms. It sustains hope when evidence discourages. Without optimism endurance degenerates into mechanical survival but with optimism endurance blossoms into thriving persistence. Thriving also requires adaptability. Markets change, technologies evolve, cultures shift. Those who merely endure by clinging to old methods eventually fade. Those who thrive embrace change as opportunity. They pivot when necessary, reinvent products, restructure models, and reimagine strategies. Adaptability transforms storms into steppingstones. Thriving beyond survival also multiplies influence because people admire not only those who survive but those who flourish despite adversity. Customers gravitate toward brands that display resilience and creativity. Investors support leaders who thrive in volatility because such leaders prove they can protect and grow resources. Employees commit deeply to organizations that thrive under pressure because they trust their future in such hands. Thus thriving expands reach and legacy. Furthermore thriving beyond survival redefines success. Success is no longer avoiding failure but transforming failure into foundation. It is no longer measured by what was preserved but by what was created despite adversity. This redefinition fuels courage because it frees entrepreneurs from fear of failure. They understand that even failure can be transformed into progress if approached with creativity. Thriving beyond survival is the pinnacle of endurance because it elevates the entrepreneur from reaction to innovation. It proves that persistence is not about stubborn existence but about relentless advancement. Ultimately thriving beyond survival ensures that the entrepreneur does not merely outlast competitors but outpaces them, building a legacy of growth resilience and transformation that will inspire generations.

10

The Cost of Quitting and the Price of Endurance

In the world of business every decision carry weight yet no decision holds as much power over the destiny of an entrepreneur as the choice to quit or to endure. Quitting often appears as the easier route, a way to escape mounting stress, dwindling resources, and overwhelming uncertainty, but the ease of quitting is deceptive. It comes wrapped in the comfort of relief but hidden behind that comfort is the heavy burden of regret. To quit is to trade the potential of tomorrow for the ease of today. The cost of quitting is rarely calculated in the moment because the entrepreneur feels only the sharp sting of failure pressing down upon them, but years later the mind replays the abandoned vision, the halted pursuit, the opportunities left unexplored, and that is when the true cost of quitting comes alive. It is not measured merely in lost revenue or unrealized profit; it is measured in lost identity, unfulfilled potential, and the void that lingers when a dream is abandoned before its time. Endurance, on the other hand, demands payment upfront. It charges sleepless nights, relentless problem solving, endless patience, and a willingness to suffer through prolonged discomfort. The entrepreneur who endures does not escape pain but instead embraces it as part of the journey, transforming hardship into tuition for mastery. The price of endurance is high but unlike the hidden debt of quitting, endurance brings dividends that compound with time. Every obstacle overcome builds not just a business but a stronger mind, a sharper instinct, a more resilient spirit. The entrepreneur learns to survive what once felt impossible and in doing so becomes capable of thriving where others falter. History and contemporary business are filled with those who once stood at the crossroads of quitting and enduring. Some chose to quit and faded into anonymity, while others endured and created legacies that now define industries. Consider the innovators who continued to build when no one believed in them, who pushed prototypes through failure after failure until one version worked, who faced rejection yet stood again until their idea was accepted. They bore the price of endurance and paid it willingly, and the result is that their names are remembered while countless others are forgotten. The truth is that no entrepreneur escapes paying a price. One pays either the cost of quitting or the price of endurance. The cost of quitting grows heavier with time while the price of endurance grows lighter, because once victory is attained the pain of sacrifice fades but the rewards remain. In business as in life the end is determined by which price an individual is willing to pay. If one understands this then the choice becomes clearer, for quitting guarantees regret while endurance guarantees growth, and growth always places one closer to mastery.

Building a Legacy that Outlives the Struggle

To endure is not only to survive the immediate battles of business but to build a foundation that lasts beyond the struggles of the present. Legacy is the harvest of endurance, and it is the ultimate prize that distinguishes those who thrived from those who merely attempted. Legacy in business is not measured simply in revenue figures or market share; it is measured in the impact that survives long after the founder has stepped away. It is the culture instilled within a company, the trust built with customers, the innovations contributed to society, and the inspiration handed down to the next generation of entrepreneurs. Struggle is unavoidable, and many entrepreneurs collapse beneath it, but those who endure transform struggle into story, hardship into heritage, and difficulty into direction for those who will follow. A company that has weathered recessions, competition, disruptive technologies, and shifting consumer demands carries with it not just products but proof of resilience. Customers begin to associate the brand with trust, consistency, and reliability, and this in turn creates loyalty that cannot be purchased with marketing alone. Endurance builds credibility, and credibility builds legacy. To build such a legacy requires intentionality. It is not enough to endure without vision. An entrepreneur must endure with purpose, making decisions that align with long term values rather than short term convenience. They must resist the temptation to compromise principles for immediate gain because legacies are destroyed not by failure but by the erosion of values. Every act of integrity, every sacrifice made to protect quality, every effort invested in serving customers faithfully becomes a brick in the structure of legacy. This is why endurance cannot be separated from ethics, for endurance without principle merely creates longevity without honor, but endurance with principle creates a legacy that inspires. Entrepreneurs who grasp this truth understand that their journey is not solely about them. The hardships they face are shaping a path for others to walk. The perseverance they model is teaching employees, competitors, and even society what it means to remain steadfast in a world that celebrates shortcuts. Legacy is therefore less about personal achievement and more about collective inheritance. To endure is to gift the future with proof that success is possible, that quitting is not inevitable, and that vision can survive the storms of life. The struggle becomes the soil in which greatness grows, and though the entrepreneur may one day fade from the daily operations of the business, their endurance will remain embedded in the DNA of the company and in the memory of those it touched. Legacy outlives the struggle, but only endurance can build it.

Thriving Beyond Survival and Becoming Unstoppable

Endurance in business is often misunderstood as mere survival, the ability to hold on and resist collapse, but the true essence of endurance is not about surviving but about thriving. To thrive is to take the very struggles that threaten to destroy and convert them into steppingstones for greater innovation, growth, and dominance. An entrepreneur who merely survives may keep the doors open, but one who thrives uses adversity as fuel, transforming the business into a force that becomes difficult, if not impossible, to stop. Thriving beyond survival requires a shift in mindset. Instead of seeing challenges as interruptions, the thriving entrepreneur sees them as catalysts for improvement. A financial crisis becomes an opportunity to refine business models, to cut inefficiencies, and to discover new revenue streams. Competition becomes motivation to innovate and differentiate rather than an excuse to complain. Customer criticism becomes valuable feedback that drives better service rather than an attack on pride. In this way every obstacle is converted into progress, and the business does not merely endure but grows stronger with every blow. This compounding growth creates momentum, and momentum is the secret weapon of unstoppable enterprises. Once a business begins to thrive in the midst of struggle, it develops a rhythm of resilience that competitors cannot easily imitate. This rhythm is visible in the culture of the company, where employees adopt the same spirit of endurance and refuse to fold under pressure. It is seen in the loyalty of customers who admire the brand's consistency through adversity. It is evident in the confidence of the entrepreneur who has survived storms and thus fears no future challenge. Thriving beyond survival also demands strategic foresight. It is not blind endurance that makes a business unstoppable but intelligent endurance guided by adaptability, learning, and vision. A business that thrives beyond survival continuously evolves, anticipates change, and positions itself to seize opportunities that others are too paralyzed by fear to recognize. This is the stage where endurance transforms from a defensive mechanism into an offensive advantage. The entrepreneur is no longer clinging to survival but driving the business forward with unshakable momentum. The result is a brand that stands tall through decades, that shapes industries, and that cannot be erased by fleeting trends or temporary setbacks. Becoming unstoppable is therefore not a matter of luck but the natural consequence of relentless endurance combined with strategic thriving. When others see only reasons to quit, the unstoppable entrepreneur sees reasons to continue. When others collapse under pressure, the unstoppable enterprise expands under pressure. This is the final destination of endurance in business, not survival, not even success, but unstoppable dominance that turns struggle into strength, endurance into excellence, and vision into victory.